Praise for *Mediating Faith*

"Wow—this is an excellent piece of work. It hooked me and wouldn't let go (a remarkable achievement for this genre). . . . Clint Schnekloth is to be congratulated for integrating such diverse streams into a readable and applicable text, one that pushes the conversation forward and is at once technological, theological, and anthropological. Impressive."
—**Ryan Bolger, Fuller Theological Seminary**

"Clint Schnekloth's *Mediating Faith* offers an important voice into a vital conversation about how new media is changing the culture, changing the church, and changing what it means to live the life of faith. Theologically grounded and richly resourced from across disciplinary boundaries, Schnekloth gracefully explores how churches can find space to share and transform ministry practice and how they might make space for silence, reflection, and deeper formation in the 'always on' digitally-integrated locales. His work will help ministry leaders to understand new media locales not merely as collections of technologies that can make communication more expansive, efficient, and inexpensive, but as 'cultures enlivened by the Spirit that serve as centers of repeating action, continuing places of possibility' where formation is richly transformed and transformative."
—**Elizabeth Drescher, Santa Clara University**

"Clint is a good writer. Made my brain sing for a while. You can use social media to reach people you otherwise couldn't. Clint's doing it already."
—**Drew Curtis, Founder, Fark.com**

"Acknowledging the spurious eschatological promises of new technologies, Clint Schnekloth helps us see the rise of new media as neither utopia nor dystopia, yet conveys a sense of urgency for the church; failing to use these powerful new medias to form faith will be a loss to the church and the world. *Mediating Faith* make a case for catechesis as digital virtual play, in which one is self-engaged and self-directed, moving at one's own pace. In gaming, one learns the game by playing the game. Should not faith formation be akin to this?"
—**Michael Rinehart, Bishop, Texas-Louisiana Gulf Coast Synod of the ELCA**

MEDIATING FAITH

MEDIATING FAITH

FAITH FORMATION IN A TRANS-MEDIA ERA

CLINT SCHNEKLOTH

Fortress Press
Minneapolis

MEDIATING FAITH

Faith Formation in a Trans-media Era

Cover design: Tory Herman

Library of Congress Cataloging-in-Publication Data is available

Print ISBN: 978-1-4514-7229-5

eBook ISBN: 978-1-4514-7971-3

This book was produced using PressBooks.com, and PDF rendering was done by PrinceXML.

To Amanda Grell,
for everything

CONTENTS

Foreword

Somewhere in the Mediterranean world, sometime in the early second century CE, someone named Mark created a novel literary form that came to be known as a "gospel"—that is, "good news." The medium used to convey the message was named by the message. Mark's "gospel" was somewhat like a biography, which the Romans were familiar with through the writing of Plutarch. It was sort of a speech but not quite. It was somewhat of a history like that by Josephus, but it was more. Just a few paragraphs into Mark's gospel, we know that we are reading real events that happened in a historical time and in a particular place; this isn't fairy tale or fable. Yet we also have the feeling that Mark wants more than to give us information about Jesus; Mark wants us to be encountered by Jesus. Mark wants us not only to know about Jesus but to follow Jesus. The gospel is a story that almost speaks for itself but not quite. It was as if the truth about Jesus Christ, the truth who was Jesus Christ, could only be conveyed through the invention of a new genre, a new medium appropriate to the message called *euangellion*.

There is much reason to believe that Mark expected most people to hear, rather than to read, his gospel. The Christian faith is not innate; it cannot be discovered by long walks in the woods or by delving into the recesses of one's ego. Someone must tell you this odd, wonderful story that you can't make up by yourself. As Paul says, faith comes through hearing. Something about the good news of Jesus Christ privileges the media of oral communication. Faith, this particular faith, is acoustical, auditory by nature.

In other words, the Christian faith must be mediated. We are not born with it, nor can we come upon it without help, nor can we grow into it without exemplary demonstration by others. Every Christian is therefore cast in the position of a receiver, utterly dependent on someone else to bring us into faith in Jesus Christ. All knowing about Christ is relational, an interaction between persons, as is appropriate to trinitarian faith. Someone must be willing to hand over to us the story of how the world has shifted on its axis in Jesus, to stand up and testify to an event that has occurred that changed the course of history. Someone must dare to be a witness and walk this way before us. All of us are Christians only through mediation.

Mediation is inherent in an incarnational faith. The supreme act of mediation is Jesus Christ. Having been encountered by God with Us, God in flesh, Christians quite naturally expect to encounter God in the material, time-bound, social world, because that's where the incarnation occurred. The Holy Spirit did not shrink from enfleshment in a Jew from Nazareth, so we are unsurprised to discover that the Holy Spirit continues to animate, call, reveal, push, and prod through human means of communication. Having encountered God in bread and wine, it's not too much of a sacramental leap for us to find God using the Internet to get close to us.

And yet Christians learn to take care with media. Not every gospel that was written made it into the canon. Not every story about Jesus was treasured and remembered by the church. Though Jews were suspicious of visual images and worried that painting and sculpture might be used as violations of the first commandment against image making, Gentiles loved painting, sculpture, frescoes, and mosaics. How curious that during the great period of evangelization of Gentiles we have so few early Christian images in the first centuries, and almost none depicting Jesus himself. These Jews become Christians were appropriately cautious with their adoption of gentile media. Then, in the fourth century, there was an explosion of specifically Christian art throughout the Mediterranean world, and pictures of Jesus were everywhere, icons too. Constantinians baptized Roman architecture, adapting forms like the basilica for church rites and the mosaic encrusted apse to encase divine liturgy.

Creative theologians like Ambrose and Gregory the Great created new music to fit the church's liturgy, as if the fine but bombastic Roman imperial music just wouldn't do for the praise of a crucified Savior. An incarnational faith seemed to provoke an unprecedented outburst of artistic creativity, a media frenzy instigated by newfound faith in an incarnate God. An incarnational faith quite naturally locates, embodies, and posits itself in human media.

The church's creative utilization of media was not without internal critique and sometimes bitter controversy. There was fierce debate over the propriety and the fidelity of some Christian media making, the so-called Iconoclastic Controversy. The church seemed to realize that media were not innocent. Not all songs and not all images could be baptized and brought into the church's worship. Throughout the history of the church, there has been continued debate over the place of media, the appropriateness of new media, and the ambiguous role of media in proclaiming and forming Christian faith. Staring at a row of defaced, decapitated statues of saints in an English parish church—victims of the more radical wing of the English Reformation—reminded me that the church has not only lived through its artistic, communicative media but has also had some of its most violent fights over media.

Marshall McLuhan taught us that a medium can change the message in subtle and powerful ways. We think we are using our technological tools only to discover that they are using (and sometimes even abusing) us. Though we presume that we have become masters of the world through our technology, we are dismayed that we are mastered. In every advance of technology, something is gained, but something is usually lost as well, and the loss may be an essential aspect of our humanity. Media are not innocent conveyors of information.

In *Mediating Faith*, Clint Schnekloth continues, extends, and enriches the church's debates over the media of *euangellion*. Although Clint is generally enthusiastic about the rise of new communicative media, seeing these as potential extensions of the church's catechetical, evangelical, and apologetic tasks, he is far from uncritical about our trans-media era. While he boldly claims that much of the new media can be signs of "the cooperation of the Holy Spirit with neurology," Clint also knows that media are never passive, neutral conduits for human communication. Neither dystopian nor utopian, *Mediating Faith* draws on some of the most perceptive psychosocial commentators on media and technology and puts them in conversation with classical Christian theology, particularly Christian trinitarian pneumatology. Clint encourages the church to critically embrace the new media by desacralizing media and by making media subservient to our theological commitments.

Because Clint is a Lutheran, he knows the radical way the grace of God devastates our vain human attempts to get to God. Clint, as a Lutheran, also has a healthy appreciation for the way we use even the greatest of human creations for idolatrous purposes, attempting to build various ladders up to God, unwilling to receive God's radical condescension to us in Jesus Christ. Throughout *Mediating Faith,* we see a robust, thoroughly Lutheran pneumatology at work. Though God's primary locus for mediatorial work is the church, the church neither contains nor limits God's encroachment upon God's creation. The Holy Spirit's machinations are always ahead of and beyond the church that is created by the mediating Holy Spirit. In one place, Clint even says that the Holy Spirit tends to be "hyper-mediated."

Media like Mark's gospel required the church to spend centuries developing the exegetical, hermeneutical, and homiletical skills to faithfully use necessary media without having them distort the *euangellion* they were purporting to bring to speech. Now awash in new communicative media and overwhelmed with proliferating media platforms, we must learn new skills for using media without allowing media to abuse us. Rapidly developing technology won't allow us centuries to reflect on these issues and to acquire those critical skills. Clint gives us some of the essential critical tools we need to exploit new media in service of communication of and formation by the gospel.

Clint's book is one of those rare gifts: a book that comes at the right time, written by the right person for the right reasons. All of us preachers, and not us preachers alone, will find *Mediating Faith* to be a gift in the fulfillment of our vocation to pass on the faith to a new generation who, without the relentlessly mediatorial work of the Holy Spirit, would not know the truth about God.

Will Willimon
Duke Divinity School
2013

Acknowledgements

I would like to thank the following: congregations served while writing my dissertation, which turned into this book, including East Koshkonong Lutheran Church, Cambridge, Wisconsin, and Good Shepherd Lutheran Church, Fayetteville, Arkansas; the Siebert Foundation for a generous grant to pursue a doctor of ministry degree at Fuller Theological Seminary; Maple Leaf Lutheran Church, Seattle, Washington, for providing a first preaching context; the doctor of ministry program staff at Fuller Theological Seminary for their close reading and editing of the book; Paul Hoffman for modeling the catechumenate at Phinney Ridge Lutheran in Seattle and for writing a wonderful little narrative exposition of it; the Our Lives, This Text group for making the catechumenate take on flesh; St. Matthew's-by-the-Sea Chapel in Second Life for hospitality at Compline, and especially Caolin Galthie, our lay leader; Gregory Walter for frequent and essential life-giving conversations; the ELCA Clergy Facebook group for inspiration and much more; the ELCA Youth Extravaganza for hosting chapter 4 as a workshop; Luther Seminary missional leadership conference for hosting chapter 5; Ryan Bolger, AKM Adam, Mary Hess, Michael Rinehart, John Nunes and Beth Lewis for offering helpful pointers at crucial steps along the way; and my family, Amanda, Samuel, Miriam, and (born while writing my dissertation) Ezra, for our love.

Introduction

To behold, use or perceive any extension of ourselves in technological form is necessarily to embrace it. To listen to radio or to read the printed page is to accept these extensions of ourselves into our personal system and to undergo the "closure" or displacement of perception that follows automatically.

—MARSHALL MCLUHAN,
*UNDERSTANDING MEDIA:
THE EXTENSIONS OF MAN*

The night before last, in the frost and light snow, I rode my bike to church. I sat down to an Advent soup supper, sang Christmas carols, and built a manger for the baby Jesus out of beloved Bibles members of our congregation had brought from home, and then blessed the Bibles before their return to their domestic resting places. We handled these Bibles with love and care, and told the story of their origin and journey. Later that evening, I gathered with a group of high school youth to discuss the Advent lectionary texts for the week in an informal, weekly Bible study we have been conducting all semester. We prayed and then went home.

Yesterday evening I went to an Episcopal outdoor prayer chapel to pray compline. Nine people gathered, and we prayed the service and lections out of the Book of Common Prayer.[1] A worship leader led the prayer office, and members of the community volunteered to read lessons and chant. Afterward we sat around and talked for a while, especially spending time asking each other about the specific prayer requests each of us had lifted during worship. Gentle ambient music was playing in the background, waves lapped at a nearby shoreline, and birds periodically flew through the worship space. Then we went home.

1. For an online resource that prepares the daily prayer offices, see Lutheran Church of Honolulu, Daily Prayer, http://www.lchwelcome.org/spirit/office/office.php (accessed January 21, 2012).

Everything in the second paragraph above took place via avatars in Second Life[2] at St. Matthew's-by-the-Sea on their prayer labyrinth.[3] This may modify the extent to which readers consider it to have been an authentic worship experience, but then also alerts them to the theological or social presuppositions that lead them to such conclusions. Conversely, given that the first paragraph describes a "real world" church event, with real Bibles people could touch, other readers will develop another set of assumptions concerning the authenticity and reality of that encounter.

I have described these two settings because modern culture (especially in the church) has not yet thought at all clearly about the difference between the virtual and the real, and has as a result largely been blind to the effects of new media transitions as they are occurring. Although one-half of this book (on the catechumenate and bookish forms of faith formation) will make intrinsic sense to most readers, the other half on immersive digital contexts and social media is still a contested "place" for Christian formation. Because of the contested nature of the virtual context, it seems appropriate in this introduction to offer something like an extended *apologia* for virtual life and a complexification of the supposed differences between the virtual and the real. It is my hope that offering such an account will curtail the number of readers who dismiss the concept out-of-hand solely on the basis of the proposal encompassing virtual church and ministry.

Christians today are still, almost to a fault, bibliocentric. As a result, our theology of faith formation in what we tend to label "virtual" contexts is seriously impoverished, and our awareness of the effects of transitions to new media consistently leaves the church lagging behind the culture as new media emerge. To the extent that this is a result of ecclesial inattention (or even intentional disregard), Christians should be ashamed of themselves.[4] To the extent that this results from the legitimate difficulty of staying ahead of the curve on new media and philosophies of the real, the church is called simply to be more intentionally attentive. In his book *Simchurch: Being the Church in the Virtual World*, Douglas Estes writes, "The church must start now—immediately—if it wants to be a significant part of the virtual world of the future. In the United States, the church has been playing catch-up in areas such as music and film for most of the second half of the twentieth century because

---

2. Second Life, http://secondlife.com/ (accessed January 16, 2012).

3. St. Matthew's-by-the-Sea Chapel, http://stmattsinsl.wordpress.com/ (accessed January 16, 2012).

4. I am consistently surprised, for example, by the number of clergy I encounter who are willing to hold an opinion about ministry and worship on Second Life who are not willing to actually try it out before they develop their opinion.

it foolishly wasted God-given opportunities to engage those media in the first half of the twentieth century."[5]

As we address this challenge, it is wise to remember that, as A. K. M. Adam writes,

> the Web itself is not very old, and it didn't become a mass phenomenon until relatively recently. . . . Under the circumstances, it would be a great surprise if we yet knew what the digital sensorium turns out to be like, or what effects it might have on us. Results of studies right now might, for instance, be picking up only (or "mostly") the effect of *switching* from a mostly-physical ecology to a largely-digital ecology. We don't have a lot of perspective on the changes in which we're participating.[6]

However, given the ever-increasing importance and impact of the "digital sensorium," we are responsible for gaining as much perspective as we can.

Introductory Thoughts on Virtual and Real

The first task is to come to the labeling of the "virtual" context with some humility. Virtual church typically means any kind of church that takes place in digital contexts. However, A. K. M Adam's subtle labeling of ecologies as either "mostly-physical" or "largely-digital" is helpful. The standard terminology sets up perhaps an unnecessary distinction between two contexts that are less distinct in reality. The fundamental philosophical question is whether any aspect of life is actually "unmediated." Contemporary media studies would remind us, if nothing else, that all of life is mediated, and much more is media than we are often aware.[7]

Take, for example, any person's physical presence in a physical community. Although we tend to live as if we are really present in these contexts, our entire presence is mediated. We are mediated through our language and through the persona (avatar, mask) we put on for various contexts. In the contemporary social media context, we are further mediated by the ambient intimacy of social

---

5. Douglas Estes, *Simchurch: Being the Church in the Virtual World* (Grand Rapids: Zondervan, 2009), 223.

6. A. K. M Adam, email correspondence with the author, May 19, 2011.

7. Hence the Marshall McLuhan quote that heads this essay, which recognizes that media are extensions of humanity that, the longer we use them, the more they are displaced in our perception of them. Although central to the church's life is the use of media, we rarely reflect on the Bible as media qua media, precisely because of this perception displacement.

networks that update us on the life and thought of those we will, sometimes if not always, see in physical contexts. We are, to varying degrees, different people in the workplace, at home, on Facebook, in LinkedIn, or at church. All the digital sensorium does is remind us once again that we are mediated in this way. As danah boyd [sic] notes in her book "Taken Out of Context," published on her personal website, on American teen sociality in networked publics, today's teens are "the first generation to have to publicly articulate itself, to have to write itself into being as a precondition of social participation."[8] This is to say that this generation is not so much different as it is simply the first generation, and so more notable, to have to write itself into being as the first act of social participation.

Contemporary neuroscience research also increasingly recognizes that "the brain doesn't much care if an experience is real or virtual."[9] There are phenomenological and psychological modalities at play here about which I will give more detail anon, but the basic idea is worth noting. As Jim Blascovich and Jeremy Bailenson explain in their book, *Infinite Reality*,

> The distinction between real and virtual is relative. Humans contrast what is usually considered "grounded reality"—what they believe to be the "natural" or "physical" world—with all other "virtual realities" they experience, such as dreams, literature, cartoons, movies, and online environments such as Facebook or *Second Life*. This contrast allows us to avoid being mired in the unending debate over what constitutes reality.[10]

At this point, readers may be asking how precisely this conversation is theological rather than ethnographical or an exercise in media studies with a quasi-religious studies component. This introduction is laying out some preliminary thoughts on media effects that will be assumed in much of what follows. Theologically informed awareness of media effects will strengthen the faith formation practices of the church in a trans-media era. People today are increasingly aware that Marshall McLuhan was right—the medium is the message—and when they are unaware of the media effects of their chosen medium, it can corrupt, distort, or even hide the message they think they are

8. danah boyd, "Taken Out of Context," PhD diss., University of California at Berkeley, 2008, http://www.danah.org/papers/TakenOutOfContext.pdf. (accessed January 16, 2012).

9. Jim Blascovich and Jeremy Bailenson, *Infinite Reality: Avatars, Eternal Life, New Worlds, and the Dawn of the Virtual Revolution* (New York: HarperCollins, 2011), 3.

10. Ibid., 15.

communicating.[11] There is even a risk of forming people into a completely different faith than anticipated, depending on the effects of the media. That is, as Neil Postman notes in *Amusing Ourselves to Death*, "the form in which ideas are expressed affects what those ideas will be."[12] Illustrating a proper understanding of the relationship between virtual and real is one important first step on the road to theologically informed awareness of media effects.

Conducting a review of "virtual church" in this way as it relates to faith formation should also send reflection back to the many places in Scripture where presence is mediated. Some of the most obvious of these include the following: "It is no longer I who live, but it is Christ who lives in me" (Galatians 2:20); Jesus taking bread and saying, "This is my body that is for you" (1 Corinthians 11:24); and the cosmological assertion "He has put all things under his feet and has made him the head over all things for the church, which is his body, the fullness of him who fills all in all" (Ephesians 1:22-23). In the first instance, the individual speaker, Paul, is now the mediating presence of Christ in the world, begging the question of which is more virtual and which is more real. It would not be too much of a stretch to argue that in this case, the virtual is more real than the real, whatever that might mean. In the second case, the church has had a longstanding and faithful conversation on precisely how to articulate the presence of Christ in that bread, because it is not exactly clear how simple bread can be the media through which the message, Christ, can be expressed and itself be the messenger of the message in the media. Finally, in the third case, the church becomes the mediating presence of Christ in the world so that a community stands in for the one, but precisely because the one is already community. All of this illustrates not so much a theology of virtual church but rather how a conversation around virtual church sends us back to our source texts and theological presuppositions and highlights them in new ways.[13]

Or take, as a final example, the most wonderful exercise in media studies in all of Scripture: "We don't need letters of introduction to you or from you like other people, do we? You are our letter, written on our hearts, known and

11. This is illustrated by the now famous mistake at the printer's where his book *The Medium Is the Message* was accidentally given the title *The Medium Is the Massage*. McLuhan loved the typographical, lexical error so much they left it that way. Media truly does "massage" the message.

12. Neil Postman, *Amusing Ourselves to Death* (New York: Penguin, 2005), 31.

13. Much of this book amounts to cataloging the phenomenon of new ways of seeing. One must reread the Bible with a media ecology lens, and much becomes apparent that had not been on previous reads. McLuhan, watching all the advertisements across the United States landscape in the 1960s, said that "once you start seeing the world as pop, you could never go back to seeing it the way you did before." Douglas Coupland, *Marshall McLuhan: You Know Nothing of My Work* (New York: Atlas and Company, 2010), 96.

read by everyone. You show that you are Christ's letter, delivered by us. You weren't written with ink but with the Spirit of the living God. You weren't written on tablets of stone but on tablets of human hearts" (2 Corinthians 3:1-3 CEB). Paul's riff on letters and tablets and believers as living Christ letters illustrates the wedding of media and message in precisely the theological format under consideration. In this early part of the letter, he uses the metaphor as a rhetorical flourish to win over his readers. Later, however, he mentions his own letter literally and makes this argument: "I don't want it to seem like I'm trying to intimidate you with my letters. I know what some people are saying: 'His letters are severe and powerful, but in person he is weak and his speech is worth nothing.' These people need to think about this—that when we are with you, our actions will show that we are the same as the words we wrote when we were away from you" (2 Corinthians 10:9-11 CEB). Paul argues that his letters themselves are extensions of himself and representative of him, so that the distinction between the media he sends and himself as the messenger authoring the message is a relative one—and he makes this argument in the context of a letter while he himself is absent physically. This last point is especially important, if often overlooked.

Paul's example should guide us to consider something about his ministry worth emulating, namely, that a letter or other media we make use of to extend ourselves is not *about* formation accomplished elsewhere, but is itself faith formative. Churches that "get" this use digital media *as* faith formation rather than as tools to communicate *about* formative opportunities. Perhaps this is an easier concept to embrace when speaking of social media, but it is still worth noting, since in the transition to new media, the tendency is often to focus on the media itself rather than embrace the media as an extension of the message and messenger. New technologies are self-referential until they cease to be.

MISSIOLOGICAL INSIGHTS INTO THE "WHY?" OF FORMATION IN VIRTUAL CONTEXTS

Truly immersive new media, such as virtual worlds or "massively multiplayer online role playing games" (hereafter, MMORPGs) take this discussion to another level. For that matter, though not strictly virtual, yet still immersive, the catechumenate does so as well. They are, at their best, another world, separate and distinct in some ways from the "real world." In fact, in virtual environments, users often refer to "RL" (real life) or "IRL" (in real life) to distinguish between real life and their virtual life or second life. This kind of language illustrates how immersive the virtual world can be, inasmuch as language then develops to point back to the world outside the virtual environment.

In these contexts, the church needs to bring the same kinds of critical tools one brings to mission, in order to understand the context adequately. As Estes writes, "The virtual world is a new mission field. We are called by God to pitch our tent in this strange land and learn the language so that we can share God's love."[14] It may seem obvious, but clearly it has yet to be embraced as a practice. The way one does mission is by going to a place that the church, responding to the call of God, sends the individual. Few would respect a missionary who expressed all kinds of thoughts about reaching the people of the Ukraine but had never been there, and everyone knows that to be a missionary in a foreign context for the long haul, the best first step is to learn the language.

With virtual worlds, the step into the mission field is tremendously simpler and more fluid than mission to foreign countries or new geographical contexts. If one has a computer and an Internet connection, one can be on *Second Life* or playing *World of Warcraft* in a matter of minutes for free. The primary theological task is for more of the faithful to actually go there, to be, as it were, "perichoretically present."[15] Again, this does not sound like theology until and if we embrace that theology is, to a considerable degree, ethnography—or said in the obverse, that ethnography can be excellent Christian theology.[16] Pete Ward, in one of the early works in this move toward ethnography as theology, titled *Participation and Mediation: A Practical Theology for the Liquid Church*, writes, "The convergence on culture marks a significant move in practical theology. Turning to culture means that doctrine is increasingly read in and through the social and the embodied and so 'theology' itself is seen in a new light."[17] This is a way of thinking of ethnography as theological in the sense Michel de Certeau has it in his *The Practice of Everyday Life* in a chapter on "walking in the city." He writes, "To practice space [walk] is thus to repeat the joyful and silent experience of childhood; it is, in a place, *to be other and to move toward the other*" (italics added).[18]

14. Estes, *Simchurch*, 226.

15. Some consider the best translation of this term to be "circulating in the neighborhood." Gary Simpson, email correspondence with the author, May 2012.

16. See, for example, the recent collection of essays edited by Christian Scharen and Aana Marie Vigen, *Ethnography as Christian Theology and Ethics* (New York: Continuum, 2011).

17. Pete Ward, *Participation and Mediation: A Practical Theology for the Liquid Church* (Norwich, UK: SCM, 2008), 95.

Walking about in a virtual world, though in many respects no different from walking around in a physical city, does highlight aspects of walking around that we are less aware of in physical environments. If we decide to walk in the city, we probably select specific clothes to wear out and about. In the virtual world, you actually dress and create your avatar to represent you in that environment. These two practices, one in the real world and one in the virtual world, are not as dissimilar as they first appear, although the technology of the second draws attention to itself for most users more starkly than the clothing technologies of the first.

Ward offers a vision of a "liquid church." He recognizes that the way church has been in the past was itself a form of mediated identity, and he calls on the church to extend itself into new cultures and media. He writes, "Liquid church expresses the way that ecclesial being is extended and made fluid through mediation. The liquid Church moves beyond the traditional boundaries of congregation and denomination through the use of communication and information technologies."[19] How the church is mediated as new technologies arise is itself a missiological topic. Ward continues, "A central missiological issue for the Western Church relates to how it chooses to react to the mediation of the spiritual in popular culture."[20] Ward's concept of liquid church offers a third way, a way around the forced dichotomy between "real church" and "virtual church." Instead, the church "goes with the flow" of the Spirit in the freedom of God because the church is not *here* in one way and *there* in another, but is constantly extended, a flowing ecclesial life, through the mediation and participatory power of the message, who is also, in the case of Christian theology, the messenger (as in John 1).

By unnecessarily differentiating real-life church from virtual church, Christians do themselves a profound disservice in that they end up misunderstanding both contexts. The actual analysis conducted here, however, has problematized the encounter. If ethnography is Christian theology, then the kind of analysis Christians seek requires not the iteration of regular theological language in such a way as to speak virtually of the virtual church, but rather requires immersion in the actual context of the virtual world in order to learn the language, participate, and be mediated there. In this way, theology can be an exercise in a real ethnographic experience of the virtual rather than a virtual conversation about the virtual one assumes to be real.

18. Michel de Certeau, *The Practice of Everyday Life* (Berkeley: University of California Press, 1984), 110.

19. Ward, *Participation and Mediation*, 137.

20. Ibid., 190.

Additionally, and this is at the heart of this book, by attending to the similarities between virtual and real faith formation contexts via the theological nuances that arise from an intentionally open approach to both contexts, one will be better equipped to recognize the actual weakness of either formative context, discern commonalities, and celebrate opportunities. Such attention will enable the church to flow "forward" more readily into virtual environments, equipped with an awareness of what the transition to new media eventuates, while also flowing "backward" in the sense of adopting historic practices (such as the catechumenate, bookishness, and the like) that the church has used successfully for millennia as a media-rich model for faith formation. In the new trans-media era, awareness of media effects matters, including the effects of such mediating technologies as the catechemenate, preaching, and video games, because it directs us to attend not only to the effects of the media, but also the message, which is often presumed to communicate apart from the medium. Inspired by the prophetic insights of media ecologists like Marshall McLuhan, the focus on content is reduced, and one begins to move from *what* is being said to *how* it is being said.[21]

The truth is that each new medium matters precisely in its layering. Even in a post-book era, the church will remain a people of the book and host a culture of books. It will also add, and is already daily adding, layers and accretions of new media, and maintaining old media, like an ancient but still thriving *tell*. The trick in the trans-media era is to continue to pay attention to the faith-forming influence of ancient practices and books *and* the faith-forming influence of what is coming next. Part of Christian vocation is to conduct, as it were, ongoing technology assessment, as Brian Brock writes, the "systematic attempt to foresee the consequences of introducing a particular technology in all spheres it is likely to interact with," all the while interjecting "substantive theological content into concrete deliberations about specific technologies."[22] In fact, beyond simply interjecting substantive theological content into deliberations, a theological approach to formative technologies will step back and look at technologies and media writ large out of a theological perspective.

Overview

This book will proceed through a series of awareness-raising stages. Before launching into an examination of the development from book to trans-media

21. Coupland, *Marshall McLuhan*, 112.

22. Brian Brock, *Christian Ethics in a Technological Age* (Grand Rapids: Eerdmans, 2010), 13, 21.

and immersive digital worlds, it will examine analogs of these developments in sister media of importance for the church. In chapter 1, the focus is on examining trans-media "effects." Under the guise of a memoir, this chapter will look at the parallels between neuroscience insights into the reading brain and the phenomenology of a preacher learning to preach extemporaneously.[23] Brains are hardwired for speech and learn spoken language naturally, but the brain learns to read printed text slowly and only through very involved formative practices. The process of learning to preach extemporaneously offers strong parallels. Then this chapter looks at the "effect" of formative technologies like pastoral internships and the catechumenal process, initially teasing out the interrelationship between philosophies of formation and the practices themselves. Finally, the chapter also looks at how the rise of "bookishness" in the scholastic period fostered a specific culture and way of thought that parallels, in intriguing ways, the formative catechumenal practices of the early church, and how media more generally (and specifically photography) illustrates this yet again.

Although this book is mostly receptive to the developments happening in the digital, trans-media era, the approach is critical engagement, so chapter 2 takes a close look at those who have gone to the root of the technological era and the extent to which the medium is the "massage" (especially Brian Brock and Marshall McLuhan). It takes time to explore the considerations of social commentators on the effects of technology in culture. It introduces the insights of authors in the movement now called media ecology.[24] It reads the beautiful considerations of those authors who truly lament the end of an era—the bibliophiles. It engages these philosophers, social critics, and literary scholars, because even in, and often precisely through, their criticism they provide the critical tools necessary to lay the groundwork for sustained theologically informed awareness of media effects. Most of the resources in these areas of academic inquiry have only infrequently been explored by those in religious communities with any depth and intentionality. By attending to these, we will be better prepared to engage thoughtfully the immersive realities of the catechumenate and MMORPGs.

---

23. This approach is inspired by Douglas Coupland's biography of Marshall McLuhan, which he prefers to call a "pathography. "Perhaps this opens the door to what may be one future for the biography of those who create new ideas, a form in which the biographer mixes historical circumstances with forensic medical diagnosis to create what might be called a *pathography*—an attempt to map a subject's brain functions and to chart the way they create what we call the self." Coupland, *Marshall McLuhan*, 51.

24. For an introduction into this emerging field of study, see the bibliography provided at http://www.media-ecology.org/media_ecology/readinglist.html (accessed January 20, 2012).

Chapter 3 begins part 2 of the book with a chapter titled "The Effects of Catechumenal Preaching." Various faith communities in North America have adapted the ancient catechumenate as a contemporary and highly integrated adult rite of Christian initiation for adults into the life of the church. The number of persons participating in the catechumenate is far outstripped by the number of adults who willingly receive initiation into MMORPGs. Chapter 4 describes the catechumenate, with a special focus on catechumenal (or what is sometimes called mystagogical) preaching and related methods of initiation in order to give the basis for comparison with MMORPGs in the following chapter.

MMORPGs are, in some ways, the digital world's corollary of the catechumenate. In fact, they do the catechumenate one better. They attract catechumens in record numbers, people willing to give of their time, talent, and energy to be a part of the process that develops them as players. MMORPGs are catechumenal—they catechize those ready for initiation into the life of the game. They are also mystagogical—they lead those who have been initiated into deeper mysteries within the game itself. Chapter 4, "The Effects of MMORPG's Procedural Rhetoric," outlines this inculturation, with a special focus on the rhetoric of games (thus paralleling the focus on catechumenal preaching in chapter 3). Both chapters include creative riffs on recent science fiction novels that illustrate the generative nature of immersive contexts. For the catechumenate, Neal Stephenson's immersive catechism, *Anathem*, will be under consideration. For MMORPGs, Cory Doctorow's novelistic treatise on games and procedural rhetoric, *Makers*, will be considered.

In chapters 3 and 4, considerable space is given to describing immersive formational, inculturating systems. Much of the new media and social networks are, though less immersive, still a part of the total ecology that contribute to formation. Chapter 5 looks at social digital media particularly (especially the ELCA Clergy Facebook group[25]), inasmuch as they contribute to and deepen face-to-face or other immersive forms of enculturation. This chapter also looks back to the book, observing how older forms of media are not replaced but are layered over, and in that sense contribute to the changing media landscape not by replacement but by creative reappropriation and construction. The chapter returns, as it were, to the palimpsest. In the meantime, while celebrating some aspects of this layering, the earlier concerns of Brock and others should be kept in mind: "When we facilitate the expression of one level of material order, we necessarily submerge and perhaps in time lose touch with another. . . . The

25. See The Disseminary, http://disseminary.org/ (accessed January 20, 2012), and ELCA Clergy Facebook Group, http://www.facebook.com/groups/elcaclergy/ (accessed June 4, 2012).

establishment of new social and material orders always entails the subsumption or reconfiguration of previous patterns of order."[26]

Part 3 of the essay is the positive proposal. It begins in chapter 6 with an excursus that resolves some difficulties around media ecology and pneumatology. Having spent so much time looking at the technologies that contribute to faith formation, there is a danger of having overlooked Who, not what, is instrumental in creating and forming faith to begin with. This chapter seeks to spot ways that the Trinity and the Holy Spirit work in the midst of and through trans-media culture in a sacramental and mediating manner.

Finally, hopefully the excursus on the work of the Holy Spirit in and through the trans-media era will have primed the pump for the reception of chapter 7 by readers. Here, in conversation with the theology of built environments in T. J. Gorringe, three conclusions that arise out of the increasing awareness of trans-media effects are proffered that then lead back into further engagement with those media as they mutually inform and form.

First, faith formation in a trans-media culture will thrive where it attends to (and is) *beauty*, and it is a unique insight from trans-media effects that beauty is grace is justice. Second, such awareness of media effects will prepare us adequately for what is ahead by signaling the variety of ways the future is actually the present. Just as the insight of eschatology that the future is coming to us in Christ rather than the other way around has implications for how believers live here and now, so too one's imagineering about the future of media and faith formation in the future will shape how one engages these technologies now. In fact, if the church is truly proactive and culturally creative and inventive, it will, like the early church and the codex, invent or further the very media technologies it anticipates are most likely to strengthen the faith and the life of the church in its formative practices.

One eminent example of this kind of creative, Christian approach to media technologies is Marshall McLuhan. This book takes much of his work as a guiding light. In fact, many of the chapters, and the overall structure of the work, emulate the style and structure of McLuhan's magnum opus, *Understanding Media*. In the introduction to that work, the editor, W. Terrence Gordon, writes, "The book defies summary. McLuhan wanted it that way. When we are faced with information overload, he taught, the mind must resort to pattern recognition to achieve understanding. *Understanding Media* illustrates the point by its style. The reader must reach for the ideas it expresses each time they whirl past."[27] In a sense, to raise awareness of media effects (which is what

---

26. Brock, *Christian Ethics in a Technological Age*, 57.

this book is attempting to accomplish), the method or style of this work must itself not only in content but in form raise such awareness. My hope is that the style and structure accomplish that.

Finally, awareness of media effects in a trans-media era attends to the truth that Christianity really is about life together, and the particular way life is life together in this era can be summarized enigmatically in that "I am the network." Theologians of network culture have come to understand networks as a metaphor for life together and life in God. God as Trinity does life as Trinity together rather than alone. It is in and through the evocation of these three senses (beauty, eschatology, and togetherness) that critical engagement with these new forms will bear lasting fruit and carry the church faithfully into a new era as theologically informed awareness of media effects will strengthen the faith formation practices of the church in a trans-media era.

27. Marshall McLuhan, *Understanding Media: The Extensions of Man* (Corte Madera, CA: Gingko, 2003), xiii–xiv.

PART I

Emerging Media Contexts
and Minority Reports

1

Examining Trans-media Effects

A new medium is never an addition to an old one, nor does it leave the old one in peace. It never ceases to oppress the older media until it finds new shapes and positions for them.

—MARSHALL MCLUHAN,
UNDERSTANDING MEDIA:
THE EXTENSIONS OF MAN

This chapter will begin with the story of how I adopted the practice of extemporaneous preaching. This may seem an odd point of entry into a book on faith formation in a trans-media culture. I proceed, however, deeply influenced by Marshall McLuhan's approach to media studies. For McLuhan, the term *media* does not simply refer to a limited small group of media employed for communication, like the newspaper, radio, television, and Internet. Media are, instead, all the "extensions" of humanity, including clothing, housing, and in the case under consideration, language itself.[1]

For most pastors, the sermon is an ancient communicative "technology" that they inhabit more regularly than any other. It is one of the most important extensions of ourselves into the communities we serve. The unique dimensions of this medium, practiced week in and week out in a local congregation, illustrate the formative aspects of media more generally construed, and so offer an apt analog for the technologies of faith formation we will consider later in the substantive chapters of this book.

1. Marshall McLuhan, *Understanding Media: The Extensions of Man* (Corte Madera, CA: Gingko, 2003), 168.

Intimations: The Science of the Preaching and Reading Brain

I can still remember, vividly, the first sermon I preached on internship. Rather, I should say I remember vividly what it felt like to prepare the sermon, and the intense emotions and nerves that gathered around delivering it. I typed out a manuscript. I agonized over word choices, sought to align theology and homiletical aspirations, hoped to be interesting. Because I had worried over the individual words, the grammar of the sentences, the structure and ordering of paragraphs, the delivery of the sermon was closely tied to a written text. Sunday morning I read the text word for word out loud, like a poem.

Reading the manuscript aloud was agonizing, because my preferred approach to communication, in individual or group conversations, is to look people in the eye, speak freely, and not read texts to people (unless it is a recitation, in which case different habits and rules apply). Here I was, in a living worship environment, and instead of speaking freely and vibrantly, I was reading verbatim a text I had written earlier in the week. I can still remember what an out-of-body experience it was, watching myself deliver the sermon. Although I had attended many oral readings of written texts, such as poetry readings, and knew that reading from a text can actually be a legitimate (and even beautiful) approach to oral communication, I knew in that first sermon that it would not work for me as a preacher.

So I set myself the task of revolutionizing my preaching, abandoning the pattern of preaching I had received and observed throughout my lifetime. I had rarely witnessed a preacher preach extemporaneously. The majority of my experience had been with manuscript preachers. During the remainder of the internship—because I had time to do so and the inclination—I did two new things. First, I memorized the gospel lesson each week and proclaimed (performed) it, like a dramatized reading. Then, following the gospel performance, I preached a sermon working from an outline I had written and memorized. At first, I still wrote out an entire manuscript, then organized it down into an outline and memorized that. Later, as the year went on, it became increasingly easy to preach without writing the manuscript first. In fact, after a while the written manuscript got in the way, because I wondered whether what I preached orally on Sundays remained faithful to the manuscript written at an earlier date. My concern would remain with what I had written or outlined rather than what I was currently saying, as if the media in which the sermon had been "trapped" was more important than the living voice of the gospel in the moment of oral proclamation.

By the end of my internship, I had even greatly modified the outlines themselves. Instead of a five-point outline with subpoints, I would have just a few words written down in order, brief pointers for remembering the way, signposts on the road.[2] Eventually, even the outline got in the way of sermon delivery because my mind was tied to the outline, and I would worry if I had forgotten a section, not to mention worry about what to do if a new direction came to mind in the process of preaching the sermon—what does one do with that? Over the next couple of years, I stopped writing out the outlines but still developed and memorized some kind of outline sans notes for a few more years.[3] More recently I simply stand up to preach without any kind of outline or order in mind at all. The form simply "arrives" in my mind, fully formed, strands woven together from the reading and contemplation I have engaged in over the course of the week.

This is not to say that I do not prepare a sermon. I still study, read, sift, reflect, pray, and meditate. Instead, all these activities coalesce around the preaching moment as available resources to weave in. They are not required. In a pinch, I can preach a sermon on any text at any time. It is my hypothesis that I can do this because the formative work of preparing those sermons, year in and year out, and specifically in the manner I have been preparing them, has changed the structure of my brain. I have neural pathways, open connections and deep patterns established, that facilitate the form my preaching now typically takes. In other words, I could not have prepared for that first sermon in the way I prepare now, precisely because it has been past repeated preparations that have shaped my brain in specific ways.[4]

The anxiety and feelings I felt in those early experiences were the growing pains of a brain that had not yet been formed to do what it now does. The

2. I am reminded of something I read years ago while studying Jonathan Edwards, that "nearly twenty years after he first began to preach (i.e., approximately 1742), Edwards stopped writing his sermons in full; so one of the most famous 'manuscript preachers' in American history shifted in the later half of his ministry to a different pattern." Iain H. Murray, *Jonathan Edwards: A New Biography* (Edinburgh: Banner of Truth Trust, 1987), 190.

3. In fact, I created most of these memorized outlines while jogging, which probably also has important neuroscientific implications.

4. I was first alerted to the relationship between the neuroplasticity of my brain and the development of my preaching when I read this now-famous sentence from Nicholas Carr's book on neuroscience and Internet usage. "Over the last few years I've had the uncomfortable sense that someone, or something, has been tinkering with my brain, remapping the neural circuitry, reprogramming the memory. My mind isn't going—so far as I can tell—it's changing. I'm not thinking the way I used to think. I feel it most strongly when I'm reading. I used to find it easy to immerse myself in a book or lengthy article. My mind would get caught up in the twists of the narrative or the turns of the argument, and I'd spend hours strolling through long stretches of prose. That's rarely the case anymore. Now my concentration drifts after a page or two. I get fidgety, lose the thread, begin looking for something else to do." Nicholas Carr, *The Shallows: What the Internet Is Doing to Our Brains* (New York: W. W. Norton, 2010), 5.

"equipment" we make use of takes part in the forming of our thoughts. I have had similar feelings and experiences when learning to play an instrument or drive a new vehicle or acquire any new communication skill using a new medium. Each equipping requires the formation of new neural pathways. This phenomenon scientists now indicate is an outcome of the neuroplasticity of the adult brain. The consensus in much of the neuroscience community (and this is a relatively new discovery) is that the adult brain is very plastic, even, we might say, "massively plastic."[5] As Nicholas Carr writes, "The brain has the ability to reprogram itself on the fly, altering the way it functions."[6]

Furthermore, and this is central to what will be explored throughout this book, the media I used to prepare sermons, and the approaches I took to preaching, were technologies that affected the outcome. Different media and approaches to preaching would shape my brain in different ways. In fact, in some sense they function as extensions of my brain. If, for example, over the past ten years I had been in the habit of memorizing a manuscript word for word, my brain would be adapted for the quick memorization of written texts, a different and intriguingly powerful tool used by many in theater and the performing arts. Additionally, and equally important, not only has the media impacted the repeating media, the media has impacted the message itself. As Maryanne Wolf in *Proust and the Squid* notes, "The reading brain is part of a highly successful two-way dynamic. Reading can be learned only because of the brain's plastic design, and when reading takes place, that individual brain is forever changed, both physiologically and intellectually."[7] In my case, the living nature of the sermons I preach is intimately connected to the mode of their preparation and delivery, and the extemporaneous habits I have been cultivating over this long period of time better serve the nature of the homiletical task and its outcome in that they continue to change my brain through repeated practice.

Finally, according to Christian faith, all of what I have described above is a happy outcome of the cooperation of the Holy Spirit and neurology. The Holy Spirit works through means, and in this case the Holy Spirit works on the brain of the pastor, preparing it like fertile soil to be a carrier of the Word. The Holy Spirit works through means, including creation itself, and so it is no surprise that the Holy Spirit also works in and through the neurological pathways forged through repeated and rehearsed practices.[8] The surprise in all of this is that such

5. Ibid., 26.

6. Ibid., 27.

7. Maryanne Wolf, *Proust and the Squid: The Story and Science of the Reading Brain* (New York: HarperPerennial, 2007), 5.

repeated practices, inspired by the Holy Spirit, do not simply train the brain for more of the same—they are in fact generative. As Wolf notes later in her book, "Proust's understanding of the generative nature of reading contains a paradox: the goal of reading is to go beyond the author's ideas to thoughts that are increasingly autonomous, transformative, and ultimately independent of the written text."[9] What Wolf says next is how I have felt as an adult learning to preach, although she is describing a child learning to read: "From the child's first, halting attempts to decipher letters, the experience of reading is not so much an end in itself as it is our best vehicle to a transformed mind, and, literally, and figuratively, to a changed brain."[10]

The Rise of Bookishness

Ivan Illich, a philosopher and social critic (unfortunately little known outside the education community), has noted the formative aspects of the shift to "bookishness" during the early scholastic period, a period situated approximately right in the middle between the early church context and the contemporary social media era. His commentary on Hugh's *Didascalion*, titled *In the Vineyard of the Text*, examines the early scholastic period for insights into the relationship between the book as medium and faith formation. At the dawn of scholastic reading, writes Illich, an approach to letters helped form the scholastic institutions we have now for centuries taken for granted. He explains, "Universal bookishness became the core of western secular religion, and schooling its church."[11] This is the pattern for formation with which the majority of people in Western culture are still familiar, and it is a pattern for formation the church emulates in its ministries in faith formation programs. However, writes Illich, "Western social reality has now put aside faith in bookishness as it has put aside Christianity. Since the book has ceased to be the ultimate reason for their existence, educational institutions have proliferated. The screen, the medium, and 'communication' have surreptitiously replaced the page, letters, and reading."[12] Illich's intriguing hypothesis is that in a post-book era, educational institutions actually proliferate rather than die off, and this because the new media allow for greater diversity of forms than in educational systems where the root metaphor of the book is the only or overly dominant

8. Chapter 6 supports these assertions in greater detail.

9. Wolf, *Proust and the Squid*, 18.

10. Ibid., 18.

11. Ivan Illich, *In the Vineyard of the Text: A Commentary to Hugh's Didascalion* (Chicago: University of Chicago Press, 1993), 1.

12. Ibid.

metaphor. Greater diversity of media offers an opportunity for greater diversity of patterns of formation.

The value of Illich's approach lies in his passion for the bookish culture he now sees coming to an end, as well as the new media he witnesses arising to take the place of it. Without saying as much, Illich recognizes and affirms a shift to a trans-media culture. For Illich, this is "the appropriate moment [in history] to cultivate a variety of approaches to the page that have not been able to flourish under the monopoly of scholastic reading."[13] He is not interested in denigrating the rise of the screen as the dominant root metaphor for media in the present era, nor is he interested in waxing nostalgic for a bookish culture that is dying and that he wishes to resurrect. Instead, his goal is "to increase the distance between [his] reader, whom [he] expects to be a bookish person, and the activity in which he engages while reading [Illich]."[14] In order to function well in a trans-media era, people need to be equipped with the critical tools necessary to recognize the impact of the "extensions" media encumbers them with and liberates them for, even while they realize that the extensions will subsume themselves the more regularly and naturally they use them.

One of Illich's more intriguing wishes in his book is this:

> I dream that outside the educational system ... there might be something like *houses of reading*, not unlike the Jewish *shul*, the Islamic *medersa*, or the monastery, where the few who discover their passion for a life centered on reading would find the necessary guidance, silence, and complicity of disciplined companionship needed for the long initiation into one or the other of several "spiritualities" or styles of celebrating the book.[15]

Illich helps readers imagine one such house of reading through his commentary on Hugh's *Didascalion*. Students trained according to Hugh's vision would "read their way toward wisdom in an age in which new collections [of books and information] could only too easily have scattered their brains and overwhelmed them. He offers them a radically intimate technique of ordering this huge heritage in a personally created, inner spime."[16]

Perhaps it is this word "spime" that captures as well as anything what this book is seeking to identify. *Spime* is a word borrowed from Einstein, a mash-up

13. Ibid.
14. Ibid., 2.
15. Ibid., 3.
16. Ibid., 45.

of space and time, space-time, *spime*. By placing two quite different formative contexts in juxtaposition one to the other, one is teasing out precisely what the space and time dimensions of the catechumenate or online virtual environments are and signify. Illich invites his readers to attend to where they are when they are being formed, how they spend time there, what media is at play in the context, and what that time and space does to them. Furthermore, Illich brings to conscious attention what is most often lost, that there is circularity to this spime, in that one creates a spime to order one's world and learn in it, but one is at the same time formed by the use of the very form one utilizes. In this sense, the communicative medium functions much like a culture. Harold Innis, in his book *The Bias of Communication*, writes, "Culture . . . is designed to train the individual how much information he needs, to give him a sense of balance and proportion. . . . Culture is concerned with the capacity of the individual to appraise problems in terms of space and time and with enabling him to take the proper steps at the right time."[17]

Illich believes that the book functioned in this capacity for a very long time, essentially the epoch that extends from the scholastic period up to the modern period, but that we are now in another transition, after the book, into what is being called a trans-media era. He writes:

> The materialization of abstraction in the form of the bookish text can be taken as the hidden root metaphor giving unity to the mental space of this long period, which we might also call the "Epoch of the University," or the "Epoch of Bookish Reading." [This interpretation] enables us to speak in a new way about another epochal turn in the social history of the alphabet that is happening within our lifetime: the dissolution of alphabetic technique into the miasma of communication.[18]

We turn to one example of this "miasma" of communication in conclusion, as one additional metaphor for how media function both with and after the book.

ONE OTHER MEDIA EFFECT: PHOTOGRAPHY

Recently, Facebook (and even the entire social media world) became picture heavy. Facebook acquired Instagram for $1 billion. People have always been able to post photos as a part of their status updates, but the new ease with

---

17. Harold Innis, *The Bias of Communication* (Toronto: University of Toronto Press, 1951), 85.
18. Illich, *In the Vineyard of the Text*, 116–17.

which this can be accomplished and the relative ease with which people can edit images to include text overlay have resulted in many more status updates published as images rather than plain text. Interestingly, if one posts the right kind of picture and topic, one gets more "likes" than a plain text status update, even if the update is not original to the one posting. In other words, although the shift to an image rather than text increases overall responsiveness patterns (which are one measure of community in social networks), it is interaction around canned graphics and texts rather than original content. This represents greater sociality but in another way is derivative and less beautiful and so stands as a simulacrum of the creativity of vibrant community.

This is a second and equally important analogue of the changes being seen in the trans-media culture. Susan Sontag, in *On Photography*, writes, "Feuerbach observes about 'our era' that it 'prefers the image to the thing, the copy to the original, the representation to the reality, appearance to being'—while being aware of doing just that."[19] This preference for the image over the thing is illustrated frequently in people's efforts to show how "real" their communities are by shining the patina of their publicity. Christian communities are more attractive, more inviting, and truer if the images they put on their publicity and marketing tools are of a high production value. This is related to the well-known phenomenon, where an incredibly "true" or meaningful experience elicits this response: "It was like a scene from a movie." The imaging of the event lends it credibility and authenticity.

So Sontag can, later in her book, argue:

> The problem with Feuerbach's contrast of "original" with "copy" is its static definitions of reality and image. It assumes that what is real persists, unchanged and intact, while only images have changed: shored up by the most tenuous claims to credibility, they have somehow become more seductive. But the notions of image and reality are complementary. When the notion of reality changes, so does that of the image, and vice versa. "Our era" does not prefer images to real things out of perversity but partly in response to the ways in which the notion of what is real has been progressively complicated and weakened, one of the early ways being the criticism of reality as façade.[20]

19. Susan Sontag, *On Photography* (New York: Picador, 2001), 153.
20. Ibid., 160.

Sontag is exemplary, in a way similar to Illich, in that she is willing to identify and narrate the weaknesses of the shift to a new art form, the photograph (in fact, no one in contemporary literature has skewered and challenged photography more than Sontag), while simultaneously celebrating it enough to give it actual and sustained attention. Sontag, precisely as a philosopher and cultural critic, is unwilling to let the matter of photographs as a medium slip away from her, as if that were ancillary to the real matter of what images the photographs convey.

The insights of Illich and Sontag are bringing to light the diversity of considerations available as media ecology is brought into conversation with faith formation. They point ahead to later chapters in this book, which will even more intentionally consider the implications of media effects in manifestly formative media ecologies, like video games and the catechumenate. It is at this point in the book, though, that adequate space must be given to the constructive concerns of the critics. It is not enough just to admit there are a few minor problems and then get on with an optimistic wholesale appropriation of new media without taking the criticisms of the shift to these new media seriously. Chapter 2 engages these critics and adapts some of their critical tools for use in awareness building.

2

Listening to the Quasi-Luddites' Legitimate Laments

Whatever specific changes develop over the years to come, the advent of electronic media will catalyze a complex of circumstances that biblical scholars in the age of printing have successfully avoided so far, even in the face of film and video media, and the dimensions of these new domains of biblical interpretation cannot be estimated on the basis of the way things are right now.

—A. K. M ADAM, *NEW PARADIGMS FOR BIBLE STUDY: THE BIBLE IN THE THIRD MILLENNIUM*

A time-honored tradition in academic authorship is to ensure that the research undertaken includes the full spectrum of views on the topic, including consideration of antithetical viewpoints. Since this book is mostly receptive to rather than critical of the developments happening in the digital, trans-media era, this chapter serves as the critical engagement section, reading social commentators who have plumbed the depths and discovered the detrimental effects of technology on culture. To avoid setting up straw figures only to knock them down, this chapter engages three primary conversation partners who represent their disciplines commendably and make arguments that, though critically engaged with the overall direction of the thesis, still contribute to it even while posing legitimate and clarifying questions. Each author's work also illustrates here in early form the three conclusions drawn out of an increasing awareness of trans-media effects that then guide readers back into further engagement with those media as they mutually inform and form.

ALAN JACOBS AND THE CULTURE OF DISTRACTION

The first to be considered is Alan Jacobs and his eloquent reflections in *The Pleasures of Reading in an Age of Distraction*. Jacobs takes an indirect approach to the critique of new technologies. Rather than worry over the development of new technologies per se, his approach is to celebrate the pleasures of a receding or changing technology—the book. He redirects not by analyzing the age of distraction, but rather by distracting his readers with the pleasures of reading itself. He offers an alternative approach, one "dominant, overarching, nearly definitive principle for reading: *Read at whim*."[1] He is interested in media effects but reframes the discussion by coming at the topic of media effects from the dimensions of pleasure, beauty, and whim.

Early in the book, Jacobs engages some of the authors mentioned in chapter 1 on the neuroscience of the reading brain, and exclaims, "Having better understood the near-miracle of our ability to decode marks on paper, we are left with a truth equally remarkable: that some of us greatly *desire* to do so, and that some of us find abiding consolation in what we encounter when our eyes scan words on the page in those strange jerky saccades."[2] This one quote alone highlights something remarkable about Jacobs's approach, something that generally speaking ought to mark more of Christian theology—a sense of wonder. Jacobs is attracted to the complexity and mystery of the formation process that leads to the ability to read, and then travels with that interest down a road that leads to joy.

If celebration can itself be a kind of "countercritique," a method for drawing attention to the joys of a medium rather than denigrating the weaknesses of another, then Jacobs is a leading voice in the cultivating of this alternate form of critique. The result, midway through his book, is this gem: "So nothing about reading, or listening to Mozart sonatas, or viewing paintings by Raphael necessarily transforms or even improves someone's character. . . . Nevertheless . . . if you really want to become a better person, there are ways in which reading can help."[3] Jacobs quite ably sidesteps two problematic claims. First, he does not claim that art is not improving of character, just that it is

---

1. Alan Jacobs, *The Pleasures of Reading in an Age of Distraction* (London: Oxford University Press, 2011), 15.

2. Ibid., 33.

3. Ibid., 53.

not *necessarily* improving. Then second, he does not claim that reading does not help one become a better person, but offers the qualified "there are ways in which reading can help." This is subtle and wise. Media effects have effects, but it is the how and why of one's engagement with media that matter, rather than the substance, or high or low culture aspects of particular media. In fact, and I will return to this later, Jacobs opens the door for the formulation of similar sentences on other media effects, such as "there are ways in which MMORPGs can help"; "there are ways in which the catechumenate can help." Nothing will help *necessarily*, but each medium *can* help, if one gets the how and why right. In other words, Jacobs offers an opportunity to relate the approach he is taking while reading books to learn how one engages other media. In fact, in his essay "Why Bother with Marshall McLuhan?" in *The New Atlantis*, Jacobs writes, "McLuhan's determination to bring the vast resources of humanistic scholarship to bear upon the analysis of new media is an astonishingly fruitful one, and an example to be followed."[4]

Jacobs has at least two reasons for contrasting reading with the ways one engages other media. First, the kind of scholarship he and others are familiar with in humanistic scholarship is, quite simply, a reliable method for fruitful intellectual inquiry. There is no need to reinvent the wheel when useful tools are close at hand. A second, and in some ways more intriguing reason, has to do with the fact that one simply cannot study new media without reference to the ones the culture has currently been inhabiting. To quote Jacobs on McLuhan again,

> McLuhan is constantly setting different media, and different periods of cultural history, against one another—constantly using X to explain Z, never allowing Z to explain itself. Through the age of print we understand, or strive to understand, the era of the handwritten word that preceded it *and* the era of the electronic word that succeeded it. Since we cannot leap ahead of the electronic era, we explain it in terms of the Gutenberg galaxy it strives to leave behind. McLuhan's method is to explain everything in terms of what it rejects, what it ignores.[5]

Jacobs reminds his readers that one analyzes media effects always and only out of the social media location one already inhabits—because one must, because

---

4. "Why Bother with Marshall McLuhan?," *The New Atlantis*, http://www.thenewatlantis.com/publications/why-bother-with-marshall-mcluhan (accessed March 7, 2012).

5. Ibid.

that is how one is situated. All the more reason then from Jacobs's perspective to engage carefully how and why one reads, and stick with that, only approaching preceding or succeeding media through the media era he does thoroughly inhabit and have some claim to understand.

To return to Jacobs's central point, "It should be normal for us to read what we want to read, to read what we truly enjoy."[6] This is how Jacobs's approach really invites an alternative approach to the study of new media effects. Much work with new media (or even old media like the catechumenate) tends toward instrumentalization and technologization, as in "We need to use social media so that . . ." or "We need to start the catechumenate in church in order to. . . ." If one takes Jacobs's lead, however, the normal and most standard reason for making use of social media, or introducing the catechumenate should be, quite simply, because one wants to and one finds joy in it.

The majority of *The Pleasures of Reading in an Age of Distraction* is devoted to alerting readers to the various ways reading can become a chore or instrumentalized. Jacobs worries about lists like "1001 books you must read before you die," or hints and tips on how to speed-read. He is alert to the ways reading can become technologized, while simultaneously remaining comfortable with new technologies when they enhance his primary goal—to read well and with pleasure. That is to say, although he is worried about turning reading itself into a technology, he finds that the introduction of some new technologies actually enhance, rather than detract from, the pleasures of reading.[7]

Take, for instance, the Kindle. Although his RSS (really simple syndication) feed, Twitter, and iPhone make him as twitchy and deficit of attention as Nicholas Carr (of an earlier chapter), Jacobs sees how the Kindle actually promotes some of the benefits of books themselves. He writes, "The technology generates an inertia that makes it significantly easier to keep reading than to do anything else. E-readers, unlike many other artifacts of the digital age, promote *linearity*—they create a forward momentum that you can reverse

---

6. Jacobs, *The Pleasures of Reading in an Age of Distraction*, 33.

7. Jacobs's book is peppered with moments when he hints that he could chase after new technologies in a negative fashion, but he always opts not to. For example, "This is, I suppose, the place where I should insert a rant against all the technologies that attempt to govern time for us, to tell us not only what to do but when to do it; the insistent ring of the phone, the quieter but (for many of us) more frequent chime of an incoming text, a new set of tweets, more email, a refreshed RSS reader . . . and I can do that. But really, the cultivating of attentiveness has *always* been hard for human beings: as long as we have had readers we have had readers frustrated by their inability to concentrate. It is the nature of the beast." Ibid., 90.

if you wish, but not without some effort."[8] Jacobs concludes that not all technology need be considered the enemy, and reminds himself and his reader that even the original codex was itself a technology.

All of that being said, Jacobs does see many of the implicit dangers of new technologies, especially inasmuch as they distract from the very thing Jacobs hopes people will be formed into—ways to approach reading that bring them pleasure. Much of digital media captures people's attention not because they take pleasure in it per se but because it manipulates them into a strange attraction to it through "intermittent reinforcement."[9] This kind of attention is not the attention Jacobs values; it is multitasked, distracted attention.

Jacobs is interested in a different kind of attention. He wants to cultivate *attentiveness*. In a powerful section of the book where he invokes Nicholas Carr, David Foster Wallace, and other authors, all of whom celebrate attentiveness as a core practice of what it means to be fully human and fully alive, Jacobs writes, "Attentiveness is worth cultivating, not just because it is good for you or because . . . it can help you 'organize your world,' but because such raptness is deeply satisfying. It is, really, what Whim is all about, what Whim is *for*."[10] Here the reader gets an authentic sense of Jacobs as a decidedly Christian author. He engages media and media effects out of a worldview curious for what yields life, what gives satisfaction, hope, and peace.

In this vein, though, unlike some rigorous and more curmudgeonly Christian voices, Jacobs's leisure and pleasure are intrinsically Christian activities, properly construed. Responding to an insight of Paul Bloom, a Yale University psychologist, that people's primary leisure activity, by quite a large margin, is participation in nonreal (virtual) experiences, Jacobs writes, "How to explain this obsession [with fantasy worlds]? One solution to this puzzle, and one that Bloom largely agrees with, is that the pleasures of the imagination exist because they hijack mental systems that have evolved for real-world pleasure. We enjoy imaginative experiences because at some level we don't distinguish them from real ones."[11] This resonates with something I discussed in the introduction, that the brain does not, ultimately, distinguish between the virtual and the real, and it is an insight that will come around as an important category again in a later chapter on MMORPGs.

The primary approach to reading as formative that Jacobs takes issue with is what he calls the "self-improvement model of reading." For Jacobs, this

8. Ibid., 81.
9. Ibid., 83.
10. Ibid., 86.
11. Ibid., 123.

approach instrumentalizes reading and turns into a kind of technology. Jacobs is worried that by turning reading into a technology, reading becomes pedantic and focused on technique rather than pleasure and whim. He writes:

> It's the kind of thing Americans love to believe, and have for a long time: in 1835 the Christian evangelist Charles Finney, later the first president of Oberlin College, affirmed that "the connection between the right use of means for a [religious] revival and a revival is as philosophically [i.e., scientifically] sure as between the right use of means to raise grain and a crop of wheat. I believe, in fact, it is more certain, and there are fewer instances of failure." Growing wheat, converting people to Christianity, opening the whole world of literature to people—it's all just a matter of appropriate instrumentation, of applying the proper technique, of carefully following the instructions.[12]

This critique of a technological approach to reading leads very naturally into this chapter's second interlocutor, this one a theologian, whose critique of "technology assessment" in his *Christian Ethics in a Theological Age* is central to the section that follows. Jacobs has already illustrated one danger, that often the rise of technologies focuses attention that rightly ought to be on pleasure instead of technique and results. He calls his readers' attention back to the Christian devotion to what is beautiful and joyous. In a similar way, Brock takes issue with technology assessment, not because it does not have some usefulness, but because it cannot be equated with properly theological and eschatologically informed moral deliberation about technology.

BRIAN BROCK AND THE ESCHATOLOGICAL DIMENSIONS OF NEW TECHNOLOGIES

Although it may seldom be remarked upon, technology is intrinsically one of the most eschatologically conditioned aspects of the present culture. The language of technology is the new, the next. Typically, new technologies signal where the culture is headed, what one may anticipate the future might be like—and by and large, people keep expecting new technologies to offer a better and brighter future. Many today place much hope in new technologies. They hope that, on the one hand, new technologies might make them "more human than human."[13] Additionally, there is a shared collective hope that

---

12. Ibid., 11.

perhaps technological advances will allow them—via avatars or clones or other systems—to remain "alive forever."[14] A considerable portion of new technologies is designed precisely either to enhance or prolong human life, and so pertain to the eschatological realities Christian faith considers and evaluates.

As soon as such technological possibilities are introduced, attendant ethical considerations come right alongside. These attendant ethical concerns are frequently considered, especially in science fiction literature. For example, how does one think about the parable offered to readers by William Gibson in *Neuromancer*, when Dixie Flatline, a character revived in virtual space from real life, says, "I want to be erased"?[15]

Additionally, technologies are for the most part adopted according to a teleological approach to ethics. The ends—some as yet unrealized technologically enhanced optimal future—justify the means (the means in this case being whatever technological steps are necessary to get to the end goal, means often problematized if considered from other ethical perspectives). Brian Brock, having noticed these trends, has written a treatise of the first order called *Christian Ethics in a Technological Age*. He writes, "The deep critique developed here is that technology assessment is an expression of morality gone 'technological,' taking the form of a conceptual routine aimed at achieving and managing efficient material and social change."[16] Brock shares concerns with some of the great hermeneuts of suspicion in the twentieth century—Heidegger, Grant, and Foucault—that the problem with this morality gone technological is that it is the deep-seated core, not just of one aspect of Western culture, but of culture as a whole. Brock writes, "We do not simply *make* technology: it is the modern Western *way of life*. They suggest that technology assessment does not solve problems but is itself a flagship exemplar of the problem."[17]

In other words, questions about technology in this perspective go beyond simply the consideration of the effects of new technologies, and instead begin to ask about technology as a way of life itself. This is an important consideration in the overall approach of this book, because if technology is a way of life in the present culture, then the critique of technology applies not just to

13. Jim Blascovich and Jeremy Bailenson, *Infinite Reality: Avatars, Eternal Life, New Worlds, and the Dawn of the Virtual Revolution* (New York: HarperCollins, 2011), 256.

14. Ibid., 145.

15. William Gibson, *Neuromancer* (New York: Ace, 2004), 206. For another profound exploration of the ethics of avatar "life after death," see the prequel Battlestar Galactica series, *Caprica*.

16. Brian Brock, *Christian Ethics in a Technological Age* (Grand Rapids: Eerdmans, 2010), 20.

17. Ibid., 23.

new, digital technologies (such as virtual worlds), but any human modes of thought, including faith formation technologies that are not acknowledged *as* technologies. In Brock's perspective, "'Technology' is a way of perceiving all things in terms of objectifiability, material efficiency and manipulability."[18] The catechumenate, in this schema, is as much a technology as role-playing games. The concern, the critique that can be applied to both, is that technologies disregard divine action and instead automatize and guarantee things like efficiency and outcomes. This is a consideration that we will return to in chapter 6 in a discussion of the work of the Holy Spirit in and through means, but it is important to highlight now that the great danger of technology, in Brock's perspective, is its disregard for the work of the divine. He explains, "Technology is a human mode of thought that, in rejecting any role for divine action, comes to approach all things and relationships as susceptible to human ordering and management."[19]

There are good reasons why technology as a human mode of thought disregards the divine—it is a mode of thought that really "works." As Matthew Dickerson, in a book that covers ground similar to the ground that Brock covers but from the philosophical side regarding the distinction between physicalist and dualist conception of the universe, writes, "One of the great reasons for the tremendous modern faith in science is not any philosophical arguments for materialism, but simply that the scientific approach has yielded practical results; ignoring the historical dimension of spirituality and final causes, and focusing instead on the material world, has resulted in technological advances."[20] It is certainly clear how disregard for the divine or spiritual dimensions can arise in contexts where attention focused on the material and technological bears so much fruit. In a culture that values pragmatism and results, culture can tip all the way over into a purely technological mode—and according to Brock and Dickerson, is very much at risk of doing so (or perhaps has already done so).

Brock, following Heidegger, takes this analysis to its deepest philosophical conclusion:

> Instrumentalists resolve to make technology serve the ends humans have chosen for it, and humanists resolve to posit good ends. But if technology is understood in the broad sense that Heidegger has outlined, then we can no more "get it intelligently in hand" than we

---

18. Ibid., 26.

19. Ibid.

20. Matthew Dickerson, *The Mind and the Machine: What It Means to Be Human and Why It Matters* (Grand Rapids: Brazos, 2011), 40.

can legislate against its misuse. The problem lies in both positions' presumption that technology is a tool that can be cleanly separated from our own untainted essence as humans.[21]

Instead of presuming to be able to have technology in hand as a tool, for Brock the first step toward an eschatologically informed sensibility regarding technology is to recognize that "technology is not an object or a set of objects, nor a way of handling objects with tools, but a form of being in the world."[22]

Not only does technology contain this eschatological dimension; the development of new technologies also has impact on perceptions of the old technologies. Crucial to Brock's reading of Heidegger is the notion that whenever one technological expression of the material order, such as new media, occurs, it subsumes another, or at the very least dramatically reconfigures that previous medium.[23] This is the historical corollary to the eschatological dimension of new technologies, because in a sense it is a phenomenon identical to it. When the old media are subsumed, they lose their ethical import in quite the same ways as the current means do when utilized simply in service to a higher end. The danger in this pattern overall is that it objectifies the material world simply as a resource rather than attending to each material world medium as possessing moral import itself. Rather than technology serving as the liberating force for culture (which is the rhetorical stance often taken relative to new technologies), technology is, in this view, ensnaring.

Philosophers like Heidegger, and also Foucault, recognize how endemic this misunderstanding of the liberative or constraining power of technology as ethic actually is. For example, as Brock continues,

> Modern political power is novel, Foucault suggests, in its explicitly technological method of training physical habits to expedite social functioning. "For Heidegger, the technological understanding of beings attempts to make entities wholly present as standing reserve," notes one commentator, but "for Foucault, the technological system attempts to make humans wholly present as bio-power." The upshot is that we moderns willingly, but without explicitly realizing it, participate in regimens that treat us and others as part of a *social* raw material to be moved and manipulated without recourse to verbal persuasion.[24]

21. Ibid., 48.
22. Ibid., 39.
23. Brock, *Christian Ethics in a Technological Age,* 57.

If one applies this insight to the technological systems implemented for faith formation, one is called, then, to attend both to how one can implement technological systems that do not invoke or implement such abusive practices—in fact, one is called to design technological systems that serve as a counternarrative or countertechnology to such—but one is also called to recognize how deep-seated this modern approach to technology is, so much so that it is embedded in all of one's approaches to technological systems, even the ones with the best of intentions, perhaps especially the ones with the best of intentions. Having noted this, one is then equipped to recognize the wisdom of a social critic like Theodor Adorno, who wrote, "The splinter in your eye is the best magnifying glass."[25] Responsible reflection on new technologies begins with an intentional "seeing" of technology as the "socially embedded activity it actually is."[26]

In eschatological perspective, what this analysis accomplishes is to demote technology assessment, not to mention ethics more generally, from the role of defining the good, the *telos*, toward which humans are directed, and instead, along the lines of Martin Luther in his *Treatise on Good Works*, makes "ethics a mode of reflecting on God and our social context so as to remain open conduits of the divine love."[27] Brock concludes his extensive analysis of the social-critical, philosophical, and theological critique of technology assessment with insights that will carry his readers forward. First, Brock writes, "contemporary Christians should expect that technological practices, because experienced as delivering power and meaning, will tend to shimmer with the promise of satisfaction and salvation that only God can fulfill." Given this situation, then, his second insight is, "The theological task is not to renounce all modes and forms of technological rationality but to desacralize it."

In chapter 6, we will return to Brock, working precisely at his goal of "letting explicitly theological claims set the terms for a general account of technology."[28] The next section of this chapter, however, looks at the work of a final social critic. Sherry Turkle engages the philosophical and social critical concerns of Brock but does so from an ethnographic and sociological perspective.

24. Ibid., 102–3.
25. Theodor W. Adorno, *Minima Moralia: Reflections from Damaged Life* (New York: Verso, 2005), 50.
26. Brock, *Christian Ethics in a Technological Age*, 162.
27. Ibid., 179.
28. Ibid., 21.

Sherry Turkle on Life "Alone Together"

Sherry Turkle may be the preeminent scholar on the psychosocial implications of the use of material technology. She has worked for many years as a scholar at MIT, serving now as professor of the Social Studies of Science and Technology. Over the past few years, Turkle has been writing a trilogy of books, beginning with *The Second Self*, followed by *Life on the Screen*, and concluding with *Alone Together*, the book analyzed most closely in this section of the book. Turkle's overall approach has been to analyze computers and other digitally mediating devices not as tools that people use but as extensions/parts of people's social/psychological lives. Her first book was written very early in the rise of computers as social devices (published in 1984). It "traced the subjective side of personal computers."[29] The second work was written as computer-mediated human interaction was dramatically on the rise (especially through MUDs—multi-user dimensions), and in it her focus shifted to "how people see computers . . . as they forge new identities in online spaces."[30] Her third book continues a similar kind of analysis, but with ethnographic research that examines the effects of more recent technological developments on people's sense of self and relationship to others.

As such, if Jacobs was the best companion when exploring concerns around beauty and new media, and Brock a worthy partner in exploring the philosophico-ethical and eschatological dimensions, then Sherry Turkle is the best partner for a discussion of what life together as faith formation is or is not as the culture engages new media. Turkle's opening sentence of her book gives indication of what follows: "Technology proposes itself as the architect of our intimacies. These days, it suggests substitutions that put the real on the run."[31] Turkle's goal in her book is to offer a clarion call to reverse the terms, people as the architects of their own intimacies and in control of technology itself.

Turkle's attention in the first section of the book is drawn in particular to the place of robots in culture. This might be a surprising move, since robots are not yet as ubiquitous as other developing technologies (although, that being said, one should take note of what is happening with the iPhone Siri voice app). Turkle's primary insight in this section is a thesis that cannot be overlooked because of its anthropological implications: "We are at the point of seeing digital objects as both creatures and machines."[32] Each chapter in this

---

29. Sherry Turkle, *Alone Together: Why We Expect More from Technology and Less from Each Other* (New York: Basic Books, 2011), 2.

30. Ibid.

31. Ibid., 1.

32. Ibid., 46.

early section of Turkle's book goes to great descriptive lengths to illustrate the various ways this is true—especially via studies showing how adults and children respond to various kinds of robots, from Tamagotchi's robots to more advanced lab robots. Turkle is cataloging the culture's emotional response to these robots. She writes, "I call attention to our strong response to the relatively little that sociable robots offer—fueled it would seem by our fond hope that they will offer more. With each new robot, there is a ramp-up in our expectations. I find us vulnerable—a vulnerability, I believe, not without risk."[33]

Turkle intuits the Heideggerian critique, technology as ensnaring precisely because it subsumes the moral import of the preceding technologies. Human beings experience certain aspects of their interaction with robots as liberative, not noticing at the time the ways in which these illusions of liberation are in fact at times constraining—not to mention lonely. Turkle observes that with robots (and to varying degrees also with other forms of digital mediating devices), people are alone while imagining themselves together. She writes, "We are together but so lessen our expectations of other people that we can feel utterly alone."[34] The danger Turkle observes exists precisely in the way in which the new technology obscures by its presence the very loneliness one would otherwise note. Each world developing through these media is a world that compels through its constraints, where people live in the zone responding constantly to its demands, but separated from others even while they believe they are connecting.

A concluding statement of Turkle's is worth quoting in full, because it gives indication of the breadth of what she is about, and the reform she is calling people to:

> I believe we have reached a point of inflection, where we can see the costs [of technology] and take action. We will begin with very simple things. Some will seem like just reclaiming good manners. Talk to colleagues down the hall, no cell phones at dinner, on the playground, in the car, or in company. There will be more complicated things: to name only one, nascent efforts to reclaim privacy would be supported across the generations. And compassion is due to those of us—and there are many of us—who are so dependent on our devices that we cannot sit still for a funeral service or a lecture or a play. We now know that our brains are rewired every time we use a phone to search or surf or multitask. As we try

33. Ibid., 52.
34. Ibid., 226.

to reclaim our concentration, we are literally at war with ourselves. Yet, no matter how difficult, it is time to look again toward the virtues of solitude, deliberateness, and living fully in the moment. We have agreed to an experiment in which we are the human subjects. Actually, we have agreed to a series of experiments: robots for children and the elderly, technologies that denigrate and deny privacy, seductive simulations that propose themselves as places to live.

We deserve better. When we remind ourselves that it is we who decide how to keep technology busy, we shall have better.[35]

Turkle suggests these action steps not because she is solely interested in privacy and good manners, but because she believes they will address primary concerns she has, first around adequate human identify formation in an era of technological proliferation, and second around not becoming oneself a tool of the tools one uses. Turkle aims for her readers to be the architects of their own intimacies, rather than the technologies they use being said architects. The technological changes she is prescribing are the outward manifestations of the cultural shift they would both signify and reinforce.

Late in her book, Turkle offers this disturbing insight: "Now we know that once computers connected us to each other, once we became tethered to the network, we really didn't need to keep computers busy. *They keep us busy.* It is as though we have become their killer app. As a friend of mine put it in a moment of pique, 'We don't do our e-mail; our e-mail does us.'"[36] This is just one example of how awareness of trans-media effects guide people back into further engagement with those media as they mutually inform and form them. If people are not aware, they do indeed become tools of the tools they use. This is perhaps the preeminent reason why research in media ecology is such an important area of inquiry in modern academic life.[37] Lack of awareness forecloses people from developing a properly nuanced psychosocial approach to the tools they use.

Becoming tools rather than using tools eventuates in a variety of stunted and immature developmental modalities. Turkle notes that humans become used to their use of tools and robots in place of direct human interaction.

35. Ibid., 296.

36. Ibid., 279–80.

37. For an introduction into this emerging field of study, see the bibliography provided at Media Ecology.org, "Reading List," http://www.media-ecology.org/media_ecology/readinglist.html (accessed January 20, 2012).

What at first is made use of to extend or supplement direct human interaction becomes, in time, the preferred form of contact. The simplified and reduced relational networks typical of digital social media are no longer something to complain about but rather something that people expect and even desire.[38] Turkle worries (and it is worth remembering that this is not a gut reaction, but a worry that arises out of extensive and long-term sociological research) that people will begin to prefer interaction with robots to interaction with other human beings. That this sounds like the premise of any number of recent science fiction movies is no mistake, for Turkle, like science fiction writers, has her finger on the technological culture of today.

Turkle additionally observes how this ties into identify formation. Digital worlds such as Second Life offer a liminal or threshold space where users are free to explore identity.[39] For Turkle, this is not altogether a bad thing. It offers an opportunity to work through blocks and immaturities, to "practice" for real life. Without going too deep into the complexity of developmental psychology (whether adults are *mature* selves or *protean* selves, for example), it is clear that having an avatar in a digital social context is one way to play in a moratorium-like, consequence-free space. What is less clear is whether this aids in identity formation, moving "adolescent" participants along the developmental spectrum toward maturity, or rather foreclosing participants in a perpetual protean adolescence.

More than one commentator on digital selves has noted the protean nature of online identities. When one has to write oneself into being as a requirement for participation, one is constantly invited to create avatars. As people write these profiles or create these avatars, they are invited to describe not only who they are but also who they want to be. Sitting down to write these profiles, "the 'real me' turns out to be elusive."[40] Even adults, as mature as the culture might assume them to be, struggle with this kind of online identity formation. Not only that, but the technology that requires such profile writing recasts psychological developmental terminology in technological terms. Turkle writes, "'Thirteen to eighteen are the years of profile writing.' The years of identity construction are recast in terms of profile production."[41] Two things are going on here. First, identity formation is being recast in the terminology of the new technology. But then, because the new technology is the technology in use throughout the life span and not just during adolescence, identity formation

38. Turkle, *Alone Together*, 295.
39. Ibid., 213.
40. Ibid., 180.
41. Ibid., 182.

itself becomes a lifelong process rather than one (as Erikson famously wrote) that applies only to adolescents.

By way of transitioning to the next chapter on the media effects of the catechumenate and especially catechumenal life and preaching, it is notable how insights into media effects arising out of Turkle offer a way forward, as well as an opportunity to celebrate the existence of media that cultivate identity formation in community, media that equip communities to make use of the medium rather than serve as a tool of it. Additionally, Turkle's insights, not to mention those of Brock and Jacobs, caution one to watch even for the ill effects of a celebrated faith formation tool so as not to technologize the catechumenate approach. The catechumenate has seldom been analyzed as a social network or technology, let alone in conversation with media ecology. As the next chapters consider some primary texts and experiential contexts for the catechumenate, this chapter and the preceding one will have equipped the reader to observe trans-media effects in the catechumenal process, and to good result. In addition to observing trans-media effects, the next chapters continue to implement, and even expand on, Brock's proposal to let explicitly theological claims set the terms for a general account of technology, keeping in mind the legitimate concerns of Turkle while watching for beauty as it appears, in the way of Jacobs.

PART II

Trans-Media Effects

3

The Procedural Rhetoric of the Catechumenate

A newly baptized catechumen testifying

A new group [at our church] named "Our Lives This Text" was formed in order to help candidates through the progression of baptism and affirmation of baptism. I was going to be baptized, and Tim decided to affirm his baptism during an Easter Vigil ceremony. Support from the "Our Lives This Text" group was extraordinary. Group leaders and sponsors dedicated so much of their time and passion to the candidates. Linda and Stan became sponsors for Tim and me. Every week, the group seemed to grow. New candidates joined the journey and new sponsors committed to them. We shared a meal and discussed the weekly gospel in small groups. Our Sunday evening gatherings were enlightening and motivating. I enjoyed the growth of new friendships. The Easter Vigil sounded beautiful as described by Pastor Clint. I felt proud to be part of it. All candidates were gifted with the Lutheran Study Bible and the Evangelical Lutheran Worship hymnal to assist in their journey. I will always cherish and utilize these gifts of knowledge.

I became extremely nervous during the morning of the Easter Vigil. Tim and I arrived at the church around 6:10 p.m. and waited for more people to turn up for the 6:30 p.m. start time. We waited in the car for a few minutes before walking into the church. We found the commencement bonfire on the opposite side of our entrance. A large group gathered, and as the ceremony began, individuals lit candles from a paschal candle ignited by the bonfire before the procession into the sanctuary. Scriptures to honor and remember our Lord were read. The baptismal ceremony began with babies and children. Three adults were blessed with baptism. My name was called, and I moved toward the baptismal font. As I leaned down, the aroma of the Easter bouquet surrounding the font was welcoming. I was consumed with happiness and faith as the baptismal blessing was given by Pastor Clint while water flowed over my head.

—(http://lutheranconfessions.blogspot.com/2013/04/guest-post-cyndi-maddox-shares-her.html)

This chapter necessitates another brief autobiographical illustration. The story I share here serves as an important example of how the theological worldview one is trained into or imbibes[1] can be undermined by the technology of the formation process that is seeking to convey that very content. In fact, the content and the form can either mutually contribute to their coherence or incoherence. Messages can be their own kind of formation that modifies how the formative technologies a learner encounters might encounter them in the first place—and vice versa.

THE CATECHUMENATE AT PHINNEY RIDGE

During the same internship year in which I began to learn to preach extemporaneously, I also had my first exposure to the catechumenate. A neighboring congregation was in its first few years of hosting a catechumenal process.[2] In fact, Seattle was serving as an incubator for a variety of experiments in reappropriating ancient faith formation practices for the life of the twenty-first-century church. Many emergent churches in Seattle and elsewhere were engaged in various kinds of recovery—not just recovery or revitalization of the church itself, but recovery of historical practices for the contemporary church. The catechumenate is especially well suited for this kind of recovery: it allows nerdy romanticists (I include myself in this category) the ability to do emergent church mission while still endorsing Christendom, because most historical analyses of the catechumenate locate the formation of it at ground zero for the formation of Christendom (fourth-century Christianity). Phinney Ridge is simply one of the more vibrant and enduring examples of this trend.

---

1. In my own case, I am referring to some of the strict radical Lutheran theological tradition into which I was indoctrinated at seminary.

2. The pastor of this neighboring church, Paul Hoffman, is the author of *Faith Forming Faith*, which I will discuss in a later chapter. Paul Hoffman, *Faith Forming Faith: Bringing New Christians to Baptism and Beyond* (Eugene, OR: Wipf and Stock, 2012).

At about this time, the Evangelical Lutheran Church in America (hereafter ELCA), the denomination to which Phinney Ridge belongs, published a set of resources for churches to incorporate the catechumenal process into the life of their congregations. This Lutheran resource, modeled on the Rites of Christian Initiation for Adults (hereafter RCIA) of the Roman Catholic Church,[3] offered practical advice on the foundations of ministry to the newcomer: Bible study, personal prayer, communal worship, and service in daily life. It was an early attempt at describing and implementing an apprenticeship model for adults preparing for baptism or adults returning to the life of faith. During that internship year, I intermittently read the materials *Welcome to Christ: An Introduction to the Catechumenate*[4] but regret that I did not go observe the catechumenal process in action at Phinney Ridge. In retrospect, I have come to the realization that this was a mistake I was trained to make, informed as I was at the time by the formation process in which I was currently enrolled (seminary). I assumed all or most learning can come from book learning, and that immersion is not necessary if the topic of study has been encapsulated and captured adequately in book form. Somehow, in spite of seminary including internship, immersion, and clinical components, I failed to digest the obvious lesson that participating in a formation process is considerably different from reading about it.

This was the bias I had at that time, a (now greatly tempered) bias I still carry with me, that books themselves can or should stand in for experience itself as a resource for learning and formation.[5] I assumed at that time that I could read *about* the catechumenate rather than participate *in* a catechumenal process, and that the reading would be roughly equivalent to participation. Although I had an excuse (the congregation in which I was doing the internship had events at the same time, and recent resources on the catechumenate had just been published), I also did not have an excuse. I was on internship, after all, in close proximity to a flagship congregation implementing the catechumenate in a Lutheran context, and internships are designed for experience-based learning. I could have asked for (and would have been granted) time to visit Phinney Ridge.

3. The North American Forum on the Catechumenate, http://www.naforum.org/wordpress/ (accessed January 16, 2012).

4. Augsburg Fortress Publishers, *Welcome to Christ: A Lutheran Introduction to the Catechumenate* (Minneapolis: Augsburg Fortress, 1997).

5. Leonard Sweet labels this tendency "Gutenberg Culture" in his *Viral: How Social Networking Is Poised to Ignite Revival* (Colorado Springs: WaterBrook, 2012), 4–5. I am a Gutenberger who has immigrated rather successfully to Googler culture.

I admit, however, that some of my reluctance also had to do with the heightened profile our denomination had recently lent to this (in my view) obscure process for faith formation, as well as my presumption that the catechumenate included a spirituality around growth in faith that ran counter to my own (at that time) radical Lutheran spirituality.[6] I was suspicious of a process that expected people to learn and study over a long period of time before being baptized, when baptism was supposed to be about God's grace and gifting. In other words, it seemed to me at the time that the technology in place to welcome people to Christ corrupted or undermined an emphasis on grace I supposed to be at the heart of a radical Lutheran theological understanding of the sacrament of baptism. I was, in a nascent and preliminary fashion, beginning to assess the integral relationship between media and message.

The catechumenate as presented at that time (or as I understood it at that time) was also beautifully complicated. It was an entire and all-encompassing program, involving many weeks (often as much as a year) of work, mentors for each catechumen, and a level of investment in a formation process and worship narrative most congregations would find substantial. Like learning to read, formation in faith in this model is assumed to take time, intentionality, and repetition.[7] Any process that engages the whole person and a whole community in a wholesale realignment of life and faith in preparation for baptism and initiation into the life of the church is, by its very nature, encompassing, and so the idea of beginning such a process in most Lutheran congregations is

6. For an introduction to radical Lutheranism, consider this brief quote from an essay of Gerhard Forde. "We should realize first of all that what is at stake on the current scene is certainly not Lutheranism as such. Lutheranism has no particular claim or right to existence. Rather, what is at stake is the radical gospel, radical grace, the eschatological nature of the gospel of Jesus Christ crucified and risen as put in its most uncompromising and unconditional form by St. Paul. What is at stake is a mode of doing theology and a practice in church and society derived from that radical statement of the gospel. . . . I do want to pursue the proposition that Lutheranism especially in America might find its identity not by compromising with American religion but by becoming more radical about the gospel it has received. That is to say, Lutherans should become radicals, preachers of a gospel so radical that it puts the old to death and calls forth the new, and practitioners of the life that entails "for the time being." Gerhard Forde, "Radical Lutheranism," *Lutheran Quarterly*, http://www.lutheranquarterly.com/uploads/7/4/0/1/7401289/radical_lutheranism.pdf (accessed April 4, 2010). I have written elsewhere on Forde's systematic approach to forming "radical Lutheran" preachers in Clint Schnekloth, "On Reading Forde's Sermons," *Lutheran Forum* (Spring 2011).

7. See Maryanne Wolf, *Proust and the Squid: The Story and Science of the Reading Brain* (New York: HarperPerennial, 2007), 19. "If there are no genes specific only to reading, and if our brain has to connect older structures for vision and language to learn this new skill, every child in every generation has to do a lot of work." Much the same could be said about faith formation.

intimidating, especially when the initial benchmark is identifying adults who have not yet been baptized who are interested in preparing for baptism.[8]

It further complicated matters that this was also the year when I read Alasdair MacIntyre. The confluence of my reading habits and the experiential learning of my internship context resulted in a kind of practical and theological "schizophrenia" from which I am still recovering. Some of that schizophrenia is exhibited in how this book is proceeding. To oversimplify, MacIntyre, in a series of seminal books (*After Virtue, Whose Justice? Which Rationality?*, and *Three Rival Versions of Moral Inquiry*), argues that all forms of virtue or ethical life are situated within specific traditions and are shaped by the habits. "Moral goods" arise within a community of practice.[9] This understanding of the embeddedness of moral goods within a place of traditioned communal practices is quite different from other rival understandings of the location of ethics, such as a deontological approach that emphasizes moral obligations or a utilitarian approach that emphasizes the consequences of actions. MacIntyre's understanding of action and practices arises out of his deeper philosophical notion that who we are is shaped by where we come from. He writes, "What I am therefore, is in key part what I inherit, a specific past that is present to some degree in my present."[10]

Although much of the catechumenal process as designed and implemented predates twentieth century reflection on virtue ethics, it is likely influenced by an Aristotelian worldview, and so it is not surprising that the approach taken to faith formation in this early period in the church's life is modeled after and informed by an understanding of moral formation that assumes a community of practice as integral for formation of individuals. This stands, unfortunately, in contradistinction to the habits of the North American Lutheran community. Lutherans emphasize life together as the body of Christ, but much of our faith formation curriculum is premised on culturally popular notions of the autonomous status of the individual. Furthermore, the radical Lutheran theology I was imbibing while on internship and at seminary emphasized the dangers of all forms of religion or moral habits that imply climbing a ladder toward God. Radical Lutheran theologians are quite skeptical of methodologies that purport to guarantee formation, transformation, sanctification, and growth

---

8. For better or for worse, more recent catechumenal resources being published by Augsburg Fortress Publishers adapt the catechumenate so congregations can use portions of it or tailor it to fit their context.

9. Alasdair MacIntyre, *After Virtue: A Study in Moral Theory* (Notre Dame, IN: University of Notre Dame Press, 2007), 258.

10. Ibid., 221.

in grace, because each (at least from the perspective of strict radical Lutherans) disregards a core slogan of Lutheran theology: *simul iustus et peccator*.[11]

The irony of such claims is readily apparent, for in order to come to a solidly radical Lutheran position, one must be formed and trained in such a position. I regret that the tension between these two theological motifs kept my participation in the catechumenal process at Phinney Ridge at "second-hand," but blame no one but myself for going the "bookish" rather than the immersive route.[12] Perhaps this book is simply one long exercise in making up for that early failure.

In spite of the fact that I never did visit or participate in a catechumenal process at Phinney Ridge that year, somehow consideration of processes like the catechumenate have remained germane to my thinking. I regularly analyze to what extent the core practices of the church where I currently serve as pastor form people in faith, noting the failures and celebrating the successes of diverse practices and approaches. I have read deeply in the history and development of the catechumenate, always keeping the proper tensions in mind. Perhaps I can most succinctly indicate my *habitus* by saying that, as much as I believe that we can grow in faith, hope, and love, this work accomplished by the Holy Spirit is always simultaneously masked by the continuing persistence of sin. I will attempt to keep this healthy skepticism front and center in what follows. As interesting as formative practices are, they do not guarantee everything, and even the most formed among us still fall into sin so frequently and in so many ways often unknown to us that to elevate what has been accomplished through formation beyond a proper level will be circumspect. All of that said, faith really is formed. Brains and hearts are changed. It is simply important to keep the very real eschatological tensions of what one is studying in mind as one studies them and remember that *abusus non tollit usus* ("the abuse does not disallow the proper use"). Just because certain approaches to faith formation can be misconstrued into various types of overrealized eschatology, this does not mean that every approach does so.

Two steps are necessary before moving forward. In addition to being as accurate as possible in describing the catechumenate as most churches are seeking to restore it, one also needs to examine the history and authenticity

11. This slogan states that in this life, one is always simultaneously saint and sinner, saint inasmuch as one is already and completely justified before God for Christ's sake, sinner inasmuch as one continues to sin and turn away from God. The first point is a theological proclamatory commitment. The second is an empirical observation and truth.

12. This paper will have recourse in just a moment to reflect on another and more positive definition of *bookish*.

of the catechumenate itself. There is at least some scholarship that indicates that the catechumenal model is itself an idealized "virtual" model for ministry. The work of Philip Maxwell Johnson, Paul F. Bradshaw, and others who have examined the origins of the catechumenate is especially intriguing. Much of that work has been toward the purpose of restoration (or perhaps revitalization) of rites of Christian initiation for adults. This scholarship has then led to ecclesial proposals and structures for implementing the catechumenate in local contexts. In addition to the widely implemented Roman Catholic version, the RCIA, there is also a North American Forum on the Catechumenate,[13] and many mainline denominations are exploring ways of redeveloping this lost art. A process like the catechumenate, in some form or another, has an appeal. It is deeply social, beautiful in its implementation, and eschatologically realistic and anticipatory.

In my own theological worldview, I have experienced conflict between, on the one hand, one kind of training that equipped me as a theologian with critical tools ready to tease apart the (sometimes) romantic and overly wishful thinking relative to this formative tool, and on the other hand, a hunger for some form of authentic formative practice that really did bring Christians into community and form them in faith. The ELCA is at a place now where it is revisiting the concept of the catechumenate. The first set of resources did not "take off" in ELCA churches, and so the catechumenate has remained a largely untapped resource. The new question, which the ELCA publishing house and some congregations are exploring, is whether a church can do "cut-and-paste" catechumenate, or whether it is the in-depth immersive and communal liturgical process itself that accomplishes the kind of formation the catechumenal process has as its goal. In other words, is the message conveyable across various media, and can it be disassembled and offered in parts, or is the media itself integral to the message that is communicated? Here already there are parallels to the analogue mentioned above concerning formation into a certain approach to preaching. One additional question is perhaps the most controversial: If the catechumenate as it is being recovered is itself based on a recovery and was designed to buttress (or even to a certain degree mythologize) an already deconstructing church, how is an examination of the catechumenate from a trans-media perspective helpful as the ELCA imagines how this "virtual" ritual and catechetical world is implemented in congregational life?

13. North American Association for the Catechumenate, http://www.catechumenate.org/ (accessed September 5, 2012).

THE CATECHUMENATE ITSELF

The catechumenate, although it is a devotional practice, a pedagogical methodology, and a process of faith formation, is, in the strict sense, first of all a medium. It is a kind of procedural media. This chapter is approaching the catechumenate especially as a medium, looking at its trans-media effects. Much academic literature comes at the catechumenate from specialized areas of study such as liturgics, pedagogy, theology, or ecclesiology. These are worthwhile approaches for inquiry. However, very little has been written on the catechumenate from a strictly media studies perspective, and since it is the overall thesis of this book that theologically informed awareness of media effects will strengthen faith formation practices in the church, inquiries into the ecological implications of the catechumenate as media should also bear fruit.

RCIA (the catechumenate) was an intrinsic part of the liturgical renewal movement of the last century. Roman Catholics led the way, when in 1972 the Vatican promulgated the RCIA.[14] This promulgation served both as a massive retrieval of an ancient practice and as a reintroduction and reframing of then current faith formation practices in parishes. Although the initial promulgation was focused as a collection of resources and rites, it was from the very beginning intended as much more than that. In his book *Augustine and the Catechumenate*, William Harmless explains:

> The RCIA is much more than a collection of rites and rubrics; it is ultimately a pastoral statement that re-envisions both the mission and character of Christian community. Not only does it resurrect ancient rituals, practices and stages. It also attempts to retrieve an ancient and quite radical vision of the Church—one which places conversion at the heart of things, which reshapes community roles, which radically redefines the meaning of catechesis, and which sees baptism as the taproot and catalyst for life-long transformation.[15]

Since that moment of retrieval in the Roman Catholic Church, many other churches have begun to initiate retrieval of the ancient catechumenate. Various denominations have developed their own sets of resources, and many individual parishes have begun to conduct the catechumenate in their congregations, typically culminating in the Easter Vigil. The ELCA's most recent denominational resource is *Go Make Disciples: An Invitation to Baptismal Living*.

14. International Commission on English in the Liturgy, *The Rite of Christian Initiation of Adults*, rev. ed. (Collegeville, MN: Liturgical Press, 1988).

15. William Harmless, *Augustine and the Catechumenate* (Collegeville, MN: Liturgical Press, 1995), 9.

Like the Roman Catholic RCIA, the volume is a set of resources that if implemented in congregations would result in the reenvisioning of the mission and character of Christian community.

Surprisingly, given how historically important the catechumenate was, and how significant the reinstatement of it has been in Roman Catholic communities, the catechumenate remains largely unknown in many North American congregations. Therefore, a brief description is in order. Craig Satterlee, in his monograph on *Ambrose of Milan's Method of Mystagogical Preaching*, offers a concise and informative description:

> The R.C.I.A. is not so much a rite as a process consisting of four periods of time that are linked to one another by three liturgical steps. It begins with a period of evangelization and precatechumenate of no fixed duration or structure, during which there is a dialogue between the local church and the inquirer. Candidates are accepted into the catechumenate itself only when they are judged to have attained a basic grounding in Christian teaching, the beginnings of faith, and a commitment to a changed way of life, and a liturgical rite is provided for this step.

This second period may last for several years and consists of formation and maturation through teaching, the support of others in the Christian life, regular participation in the Church's worship, and active involvement in the Church's mission. Several liturgical rites are provided for use during this time. Particularly noteworthy is the expectation that the catechumens will generally be dismissed during worship before the celebration of the Eucharist begins as a public sign of their status as not yet fully initiated into Eucharistic fellowship.

When those responsible for the catechumens' formation determine that they are ready, the catechumens may proceed to the third stage, known as the period of purification and enlightenment. This period usually coincides with Lent and is intended as a time of spiritual recollection. The entire local church is involved in the rite of election or enrollment of names on the first Sunday of Lent, which constitutes the liturgical step in this period and is presided over by the bishop. Other rites assigned to this period include public scrutiny and exorcism on the third, fourth, and fifth Sundays and celebrations in which the candidates are formally presented with the Creed and Lord's Prayer and subsequently expected to recite them back.

The third liturgical step, the sacraments of initiation themselves—baptism, confirmation, and the Eucharist—will then normally take place during the

Easter Vigil, though some preparatory rites may be done at an earlier assembly of the elect on Holy Saturday. The final stage in the process is the period of *mystagogia*, or postbaptismal catechesis, which extends throughout the Easter season.[16]

Even this short description gives a sense of the media-intensive nature of the catechumenal process. Groups read the Bible together in face-to-face small groups. Leaders implement curricular material. Pastors preach. Presiders lead worship, baptize, and commune. However, as will be discussed in the next chapter on MMORPGs, there is also another medium at work in the catechumenate that may be less noted precisely because it is not something typically categorized as media. The catechumenal process is implicitly a procedural rhetorical structure, and so the design of the process is integral to its rhetorical power. What makes the catechumenate especially intriguing but also challenging is that it cannot be laid out as a kind of formulaic curriculum like many school curriculums. Although there is an overall structure to it, with constitutive parts like stages of inquiry, exploration, intense preparation, and baptismal living[17] (or as Paul Hoffman describes it, inquiry, catechumenate, baptismal preparation, and baptismal living, sometimes called *mystagogy*),[18] it is, as it were, demonstratively more of an overall shift in culture shaped by a procedural communal medium. Hoffman writes, "Among the hardest concepts to grasp for those new to the adventure of catechumenal ministry is that it is oral, relational, and without an off-the-shelf curriculum. Just as we believe that all liturgy is local, so we believe that the practice of the catechumenate is local. It is parish-based, person-to-person, and highly driven by laypersons, not pastors."[19] Note that Hoffman calls it the "practice" of the catechumenate. This distinction is important. The catechumenate functions as it does because it is a practice that weaves together a variety of media strands.

This particular practice, the catechumenate, is also a grammar. The procedures and process teach the language of faith. They do not simply inform; they form individuals and communities in shared discourse and language structures. Harmless writes:

16. Craig Satterlee, *Ambrose of Milan's Mystagogical Preaching* (Collegeville, MN: Liturgical Press, 2002), 5.

17. Augsburg Fortress Publishers, *Go Make Disciples: An Invitation to Baptismal Living* (Minneapolis: Augsburg Fortress, 2012), 23.

18. Hoffman, *Faith Forming Faith*, 7.

19. Ibid., 31.

For Catholic Christians, sacraments are essential elements for the grammar of faith. And this grammar, like that of any language, generally works beneath the surface: mediating meanings, establishing canons of intelligibility, structuring what is expressible and what is not. Because of this grammatical shift, we may more readily recognize confirmation's baptismal moorings and begin to savor and prove its messianic and pneumatic themes.[20]

The catechumenate, in comparison to other models of faith formation, is particularly rich at this point because it encompasses an array of media, including Scripture, preaching, sacraments, music, and repetition of habitual actions and practices.

The catechumenate is inexhaustibly rich and in some ways is better experienced than written about. In what follows, the focus is on two aspects of the catechumenate that are especially pertinent to an understanding of their media effects. First, the narrative of bringing the catechumenate to a specific congregation—Phinney Ridge Lutheran Church in Seattle, Washington—to illustrate how an immersive process like the catechumenate reconfigures much more than just faith formation processes for those involved in the catechumenate in the parish. Embedded in this section will be some reflection on the shape of preaching (mystagogy) in the catechumenal process, noting how this one (oral) medium is formed and informed by its contextualization in a larger procedurally rhetorical reality. Then a conclusion reviewing some literature that indicates that perhaps the catechumenate is (at least in part) a "fabrication." If this is true, it may be less that it undermines the value or trustworthiness of the catechism, but rather simply highlights, as emphasized in the introduction to this book, that the distinction between the virtual and the real is never as stark as we think, and a virtual proposal for a catechumenate can have real results.

Liturgy Is Its Own Best Catechesis

Liturgy is its own best catechesis.[21] There seems to be something endemic to late modern thought that makes it very difficult culturally to recognize or embrace this truth. Somehow the present culture has developed a quasi-gnostic notion that catechesis is about, primarily, cognition. One has been catechized

---

20. Harmless, *Augustine and the Catechumenate*, 13.

21. This will be exemplified even more transparently in the next chapter on massively multi-player role-playing games. In such games, the liturgy/game is literally its only form of catechesis.

when one *understands* something. Under this system, almost all approaches to the catechumenate take a cognitive approach, imparting to the catechumens bodies of knowledge. Many confirmation programs in congregations unfortunately are shaped this way. They make the youth memorize the catechism, learn content, and read packages of information. Although (fortunately) newer research into teaching methodology has relieved this problematic system somewhat, it still remains the dominant assumption in many Christian contexts. In fact, sometimes access to the sacraments or liturgy themselves are restricted until *understanding* happens.

In this decidedly modern scenario, entrance to the sacraments is adjudicated not on sacramental but rather on cognitive scientific grounds. Children become full members of the church when they assent to a body of doctrine. Or children can receive communion when they rightly discern Christ present. Or churches practice believers' baptism. By comparison, in a faith formation process that views liturgy itself as media and looks for the ways in which liturgy is its own best catechesis, preparation for the sacraments of the liturgy is enacted in the process of participating in the liturgy itself. It is not that understanding or belief are separated from catechesis and liturgy, but rather that they are embedded in, and become part of, these larger procedural realities. Liturgy as catechesis makes sense then because it takes liturgy for what it actually is—formation—and it approaches entrance to the various rites of the church from a decidedly sacramental and theological perspective.

Moreover, such an approach to liturgy and sacraments is also simply good pedagogy. Take, for example, the still common yet problematic practice of withholding communion from children until the "age of reason." Maxwell Johnson, in a section of his book on the RCIA titled "An Advocacy for and the Practice of the Communion of All the Baptized," writes:

> It is precisely within what some have called the "first stage of faith," that is, ages two to six, where children possess the greatest and most lasting responsiveness to images, rituals, and symbols. Given this, it should become increasingly clear as well that the denial of the Eucharist to the youngest of baptized children is nothing other than the denial of the *primary* way in which they actually *can* participate in the symbolic, ritual, and image-laden liturgical self-expression of the faith community.[22]

22. Maxwell Johnson, *The Rites of Christian Initiation: Their Evolution and Interpretation* (Collegeville, MN: Liturgical Press, 1999), 374–75.

Perhaps a comparison (anticipating chapter 4) is in order. Very few adults, if any, require that children read the entire manual for a video game before playing it, nor is it a precondition of using a gaming console that children understand fully how the console works, where it came from, and what the historical developments were that led up to the specific console in question. In fact, most adults would find such expectations decidedly absurd. They intuit rightly that the way to learn a game is to play a game. The way to learn how to use a digital device is to use it. But for some reason, when it comes to specific church "technologies," suddenly things like assent, comprehension, and so on, are required not as part of what goes on while engaging the technologies, but rather as access to the technologies themselves. It is as if in the church children are told that they cannot have books until they learn how to read.

Paul Hoffman, when he accepted the call to Phinney Ridge Lutheran Church fifteen years ago, recognized that the congregation had been preparing, and he had been preparing himself, to make some shifts in church culture that were more aware of the problems inherent in this misuse of media in the church. The church he was called to pastor was designed to meet the needs and cultural context already quickly receding. Seattle was becoming increasingly secular, multicultural, and multireligious. Hoffman writes, "Ministering in one of the most unchurched cities of the United States, Phinney Ridge Lutheran congregation [was] discover[ing] a way that opens the airways for the breath of God to blow through the dry, dry valley of a postmodern church in Seattle, Washington, and bring that church to life."[23]

In his book, Hoffman takes time to describe the slow and patient approach he has taken, over many years, to implement a catechumenal process like the one described by Satterlee above in his congregation. Because as a congregation they are always preparing for, or are already engaged in, a catechumenal process, they are constantly thinking through how to invite new participants in, how to form faith in those currently participating, and how this process fits or meshes with wider congregational life. Hoffman believes that the catechumenate is itself not simply a model that helps those participating to come to deeper and more sustaining faith. He also sees how the model as it is embedded in congregational ministry strengthens and changes the congregation as a whole. He writes, "Our catechumenal story is the story of how, through the baptismal preparation of new Christians, *we as a congregation* are formed in faith and strengthened for mission in the world, over and over again."[24]

23. Hoffman, *Faith Forming Faith*, xix.
24. Ibid., 5.

The overall approach is in many ways consonant with some of the pedagogical strategies of gaming culture that will be examined in the next chapter. Learners have considerable input into the process. Even the stages and how quickly they go through them are defined by those inquiring, not by those in leadership.[25] Fundamental to what they do week in and week out is this: "For [an] hour, led by a lay Bible study leader, small groups of six to eight persons meet in separate rooms. The pastors do not participate, nor do they visit these groups. The topic at hand is the Gospel text from the morning's liturgy and the sermon."[26] Anyone familiar with weekly church ministry and small group ministry will find nothing new here. However, it is the specific ways this format is nuanced that give it its immersive and rhetorical power. Because it is based on the Sunday liturgical texts and sermons, it is media rich. Because it meets in small groups but without the participation of a pastor, it can be focused on the questions of the participants and formation together as a lay community rather than "downloading" information from the pastor. Finally, because there is not a curriculum, but only the Bible and a group of people and the Sunday worship, the model itself is highly adaptable to local context, mobile, and simple.

Phinney Ridge calls this process "the WAY." It is difficult to overstate how important it is to them to describe the catechumenate as a journey of inquiry and into deeper community. Hoffman writes, "The WAY's gift is first and foremost the assurance that baptism is incorporation into a community of Christ. This community *continues* to struggle, doubt, question, and discern how the ancient words of Scripture and the Spirit of the resurrected Jesus among us equip us for witness in the world."[27] The groups function something like a living "Wiki," each participant contributing something to the WAY. It is, as it were, an open-source faith formation process.

In addition, like any good video game or any great artistic process, Hoffman's description of the WAY at Phinney Ridge illustrates that a process is, after all, a process. There is an art to it, and often one figures it out as one goes. Hoffman continues:

> One of the true blessings and gifts of catechumenal practice is its adaptability and flexibility to the particular circumstances within one's parish and to the special needs of those who participate in the annual walk toward baptism or its affirmation. With a creative imagination and a pastoral ear and eye tuned to the needs of both

25. Ibid., 8.
26. Ibid., 9.
27. Ibid., 14.

parish and Christian apprentice, there are few limits on what is possible in bringing people into the welcoming arms of a loving Christ.[28]

To anticipate the next chapter a bit, it is remarkable how similar this description of the catechumenate at Phinney Ridge is to descriptions of the popular role-playing game The Elder Scrolls V: Skyrim. A factor that contributes immensely to the popularity of this game (and others like it) is that players can play the game as narrated, they can depart the narrative, or they can flow back and forth into and out of the narrative, in this way making individual and flexible something that is also communal and singular.

Mystagogical Preaching in the Catechumenate

The catechumenate "mods" other practices in the church, and nowhere is this more apparent than in its modification of preaching. Whereas much of preaching is cognitive and instructional in nature, mystagogical preaching and teaching "has as its goal conveying a vision of the sacraments to the church that both shapes and enlivens it."[29] In other words, while maintaining a commitment to orality, mystagogical preaching is decidedly visual, casting a vision and proclaiming sacramental realities. However, instead of simply conveying information or equipping hearers with rational tools for analyzing texts, mystagogical preaching is more like a training ground for practicing Christians. Mystagogical preaching, one might say, is geared more toward practice than comprehension. Satterlee writes:

> Ambrose did not emphasize that the candidates need to correctly understand the Creed but that they recite it daily in order to enjoy its power to ward off shocks to mind and body and to shield them from temptation. In all these ways, the purpose of preparation for participation in the rites was not to ensure that candidates for baptism correctly comprehended the meaning of the sacraments but to make certain that, like athletes, they follow a rigorous discipline of daily

---

28. Ibid., 70.

29. Satterlee, *Ambrose of Milan's Mystagogical Preaching*, xxiii. Satterlee continues, "Mystagogy is sustained reflection on the Church's rites of initiation, preaching on the 'mysteries' of the Christian faith. Mystagogy is scripturally based, takes place within a liturgical setting, is addressed exclusively to the Christian community, and has as its goal the formation *of* Christians rather than providing religious information *to* Christians" (p. 9).

training in order to be in shape to participate in both the rites and the new life that flows from them.[30]

Harmless, in a book to which Satterlee's work on Ambrose is a companion volume, adds, "The catechumenate is not a school, but an initiation: the school has some students who learn a lesson; initiation has some disciples who discover a life."[31]

In other words, those who work to make the catechumenate a more integral part of church life do so because they see that the technology (the rite of Christian initiation) itself, when done well, eventuates in a completely different, life-transforming mode of formation than more typical "modern" approaches to faith formation that are focused more on lessons and information rather than life and formation. Although it might appear that their worry about the shape or structure of the catechumenate is an example of how we attend to new media itself rather than embrace it as an extension of the messenger or message itself, in this particular case, reasonable attention to the medium is in order because the modification of the medium is integrally related to the message itself. This is similar to Brock's analysis of Martin Heidegger, that a technology is a form of "being in the world." One might say that the catechumenate as a technology offers a form of being in the world that results in some of the immersive and dialogical patterns that have been described herein, so that the technology itself speaks and teaches.

Intriguingly, however, this technology was not a technology set aside exclusively for catechumens. Instead, it was (and remains) highly integrated with the overall liturgical and catechetical practices of most congregations. At the point catechumens would enter the actual catechumenal process, they would in a sense disappear into the congregation as a whole. They did not receive special instruction at this point. Harmless writes, "Instead catechumens seem to have simply blended in with the baptized, with penitents, with any who might attend the Liturgies of the Word. There all would have pondered the same Scriptures, sang the same psalms, heard the same sermons. In other words, what catechumens heard did not seem to have differed from what other groups in the assembly heard."[32] Because of this, some scholars of the catechumenate have assumed this meant churches in and around the period of Augustine had no catechumenate at all. However, Harmless notices, in his reading of the sermons of Augustine, that Augustine periodically calls the catechumens out in

30. Ibid., 319.

31. Harmless, *Augustine and the Catechumenate*, 17.

32. Ibid., 157.

his sermons. There is not a special sermon for the catechumens, but they are also not completely dissolved into the whole. They remain a special set within a larger set.

This observation is pertinent because it illustrates once again how closely aligned the catechumate and much gaming culture actually are. Although some games have a short tutorial at the very beginning, it is rare after that initial orientation to have special further trainings for gamers. Instead, all further formation is integrated into the game itself. Clearly, practitioners of the catechumenate such as Augustine intuited that the liturgy itself was quite like this—immersion in the liturgy was its own best formative practice. Then, in the context of the liturgy, mystagogical preaching, preaching that called attention to and layered the Word with the mysteries of the sacraments, could function well. Harmless writes:

> Augustine's classroom was his basilica; here the rhythms of education moved to the rhythms of the liturgy itself. Every gesture, every sign, every word mattered—whether ritual greetings, sitting-and-standing arrangements, the cross people "wore" on their foreheads, or the secrecy of what followed dismissal. All these, Augustine insisted, held some import for how one believed, felt, and acted.[33]

THE MYTH OF THE CATECHUMENATE

Recent scholarship into the history of the catechumenate has drawn attention to the possibility that not all of the resources that have been "recovered" from the early church and adapted for contemporary use are actually reliable. The most famous example is the *Apostolic Tradition*, attributed to Hippolytus of Rome. Many scholars, with Paul F. Bradshaw at the forefront, now argue that this work of church order is not the work of one author and not attributable to the early part of the third century.[34] This may seem like an obscure historical and redaction-critical claim. It takes a bit of explanation but is appropriate at the conclusion of a chapter celebrating the catechumenate as an immersive faith formation technology for the twenty-first century.

The main point here is that arguments for the recovery of this ancient tradition have (largely) been based on its antiquity. If it is an example of catechesis before what Aidan Kavanagh has called the "de-ritualization of

---

33. Ibid., 235.

34. See Paul F. Bradshaw, *Liturgy in the Absence of Hippolytus*, http://www.lexorandi.es/TeologiaLiturgica/Liturgy in the Absence of Hippolytus.pdf (accessed June 5, 2012).

catechesis," then it has a historical validity that will convince many church leaders and congregations to make use of it.[35] Furthermore, it then seems to be emulating a practice native to a period in the life of the church to which many are attracted—the growing and vital first- and second-century church. For example, in the ELCA's most recent resource on the catechumenate, in an essay titled "Forming Christians, Transforming Congregations," the author writes, "So what does it look like when Christian communities of the twenty-first century allow first-century assumptions to shape our process of welcoming people?"[36]

However, if the catechumenate as it is described in *Apostolic Tradition* is actually a composite text by redactors who were seeking to consolidate practices from around the region in order to shore up what was already a declining formational process, then that puts a whole other spin on "recovery" of the catechumenate and its usefulness for Christian faith formation in the twenty-first century. If what Bradshaw is arguing is actually true, the sentence from *Go Make Disciples* above would have to be rewritten to read, "So what does it look like when twenty-first-century Christian communities appropriate the collated catechumenal components of a composite document designed to shore up the catechumenal process at the height of the rise of Christendom to shape how we welcome new people?"

Bradshaw is worth quoting at length:

> At this stage you may be wondering what such an obscure academic dispute might have to do with the wider history of liturgy or with present-day liturgical revision. Far from its being an unimportant sideshow, as might appear at first sight, I intend to demonstrate that its consequences are far-reaching. First, very many of the claims that are made about what the whole of "the early church" did in its worship turn out to rest chiefly, and in some cases entirely, upon the evidence of this one document. If this church order is not a reliable guide to what even one local community was doing in the third century, but contains composite rites that were never celebrated in that particular form anywhere in the world, then this has profound consequences for the picture that we paint of early Christian liturgies. Second, because there are so very few detailed sources for early Christian liturgical practices, modern liturgical revision has to a very considerable extent drawn upon this particular

---

35. Harmless, *Augustine and the Catechumenate*, 360.

36. Augsburg Fortress Press, *Go Make Disciples*, 187.

text in order to produce the rites currently in use in many churches. Thus if the historical foundations of these constructions turn out to be sand rather than the firm rock that they were imagined to be, the effects on our present-day worship practices could be considerable. We may all need to don hard hats to escape the falling masonry of liturgy in the absence of Hippolytus.[37]

However, Bradshaw does not raise this issue in order to undermine the credibility of the catechumenate or other liturgical rites per se. He simply identifies this issue in order to indicate that some of the arguments *for* the recovery of the catechumenate are based on faulty historical arguments, even fabricated and amalgamated texts.

Bradshaw continues:

> History alone cannot settle matters. In any case, the supposed appeal to history by liturgical reformers has always been highly selective. We have found in ancient liturgies the things that we wanted to find, and ignored and passed over those that did not suit our current needs. I see my job as turning the spotlight on the full range of early Christian worship practices in order to discourage such a subjective approach and to reveal just how varied what the early church did really was.[38]

Here is what is most intriguing in all of this. Perhaps there is no "recovery" of an ancient practice, ever. Perhaps it is impossible. Instead, every liturgical innovation is a "virtual" product, woven together of various historical, theological, cultural, and personal strands. In this scenario, rather than criticizing the *Apostolic Tradition* for being attributed to Hippolytus while it is actually a composite text, one might instead celebrate it functioning as a composite text and realize that every recovery is actually invention, and that is not a bad thing.

Furthermore, one can attend to the wisdom of Bradshaw, who recognizes that there are other criterion for implementing liturgical change other than historical ones. And one of those is to liturgize or catechize "at whim." Which is to say, as informative as the historical record on this is, and as important

37. Paul F. Bradshaw, "Liturgy in the Absence of Hippolytus," The Kavanagh Lecture Delivered October 10, 2001, http://www.lexorandi.es/TeologiaLiturgica/Liturgy in the Absence of Hippolytus.pdf (accessed August 28, 2012).

38. Ibid.

as it is to study and learn from it, in the end it is also necessary to discern for oneself what will work, what is wise, what will form faith in this era. One ought to heed the earlier warnings of Brock and Heidegger, and not accidentally instrumentalize the catechumenate itself as a "technology" that offers guaranteed results. Paradoxically, it is by going deeper into what is perceived as in essence an even more technological form of the catechumenate that the next chapter goes in a new direction. As one way into a contemporary exploration of what the catechumenate might look like in a trans-media era, the next chapter turns to one of the most immersive and transformative catechetical processes of all—indoctrination into the world of games and MMORPGs.

4

The Effects of MMORPG's Procedural Rhetoric

Through good game design we can leverage deeper and deeper learning as a form of pleasure in people's lives without any hint of school or schooling.

In my view video games are a new art form. We have no idea yet how people "read" video games, what meanings they make from them. Still less do we know how they will "read" them in the future. Video games are at the very beginning of their potential—"we ain't seen nothin' yet."

—James Paul Gee, *What Video Games Have to Teach Us about Learning and Literacy*

In this chapter, in order to illustrate how precisely insights into the procedural rhetoric of MMORPGs can provide resources for the church as it deepens its understanding of media effects, I will begin by quoting at length a lecture given to youth workers for a national ELCA youth leadership conference, the 2012 ELCA Extravaganza, held February 9–12, 2012, in New Orleans. By maintaining some of the flavor of a document prepared as a lecture, my hope is that the book itself will illustrate in a nutshell how media informs and shapes message. The title of this lecture is "Virtual Community, Collectives, and Play: The New Culture of Learning."

At the beginning of our time together, I invite you to enter an imaginative space with me. Consider this possibility, that participation in the Extravaganza, and in this workshop, in fact even participation in the ELCA Youth Ministry Network, is a form of gaming. Consider.

First, the network itself is an example of "crowdsourcing." Crowdsourcing is inviting a large group of people to cooperatively tackle a big project . . . outsourcing a job to a crowd. The network has as its goal to empower and strengthen adult youth ministry leaders in service to Christ. It does this through networking youth ministry leaders serving and supporting each other. As one example, I'm here of my own free will, nonstipendiary, to conduct this workshop. All the other workshop leaders have also been crowdsourced, as have a majority of the youth leaders who plan the Extravaganza and serve in various volunteer capacities with the ELCA Youth Ministry Network.

Second, and this is more a psychological theory, when you came to this Extravaganza, you came as an avatar. You are in all likelihood not exactly the same person you are in other contexts—with your youth, in your church, in your family. Here at the Extravaganza, you are the avatar you have selected to represent yourself in this socially constructed environment, in New Orleans, at a conference with other youth leaders. Some of our avatars are quite a bit like the avatars we put on in other places. Some others of us "present" quite a bit differently here than elsewhere.

Third, our whole system of workshops is itself a complicated form of gaming. You had a map, and a schedule, and you are finding your way around this hotel seeking out workshop experiences that will gain you experience points you hope will level you up to new levels of ministry when you return home. Attend the right workshop, and you'll go from being a level 12 youth leader to level 14. Level 14 comes with a brand-new crossbow and extra healing spells.

Within this particular workshop, we are gaming according to certain rules. Some workshops have an open, Minecraft-like feel (build whatever you want, wherever). This particular workshop is more directed. You have some imaginative freedom, but I have selected a lecture format to walk us through some new territory that, *Myst*-like, might be difficult to navigate if certain puzzles or wayposts are not navigated correctly.

The Extravaganza is a good game world. It attracts a large number of participants because of the play area (New Orleans), the various collaborative and networking possibilities, and its existence as a kind of "built environment" with lectures, worship, meals, and workshops. The "E" also has good game mechanics, with variety and flow and open space to roam and explore and chill. Aspects of the "E" allow for great control over the environment, such as the early Intensives on offer. The mechanics could be improved if there were some kind of real payoff for attendance, like earning academic credit hours . . . but perhaps that is available and it's simply a part of the game mechanics I haven't discovered yet. Finally, the "E" has (and this is its greatest selling point) great game community. There's plenty of space for positive social interaction and a meaningful context for collective effort.[1]

BRINGING THE GAME

Early drafts of this lecture began with arguments for why youth workers and church leaders should game. It was my original thought that winsome and compelling narratives of the difference gaming makes might draw the listeners into the gaming world. I assumed that since youth workers are missionaries, they would be up for being sent into new cultural contexts and venues. In addition, my early lecture plans included the goal of disabusing hearers of their patronizing and ill-informed judgments against virtual worlds and the gaming culture. My plan was to use a dual strategy of invitation and attack.

Then I started inviting people to participate with me in daily prayer on Second Life. To date, the only person I have successfully convinced to create an avatar and meet me at St. Matthew's-by-the-Sea for compline is my brother, who I think, though in some ways curious, participated under a bit of filial duress. Over time, I have learned that very few pastors and church leaders inhabit digital virtual worlds, and in fact most pastors and church leaders have some rather obdurate and steadfast reasons for not inhabiting those worlds (they don't have enough time; they are concerned about boundary issues; they are not tech savvy; it is not a high priority; they just do not get it; they believe it is silly; they believe it is not real community; and so on). Douglas Estes, in his fascinating book, *Simchurch*, observes something similar to what I have experienced in having conversations on this topic at church: "If we want to reach people in the virtual world, we have to reach avatars, even though the whole avatar thing gives a lot of church people the willies."[2] Never mind, as Estes notes, that the "Christian church is engaging far less than 1 percent of the

1. For an approach to Wikipedia as a gaming environment, which is the inspiration for this introduction, see Jennifer McGonigal's *Reality Is Broken: Why Games Make Us Better and How They Can Change the World* (New York: Penguin, 2011), 230.

2. Douglas Estes, *Simchurch: Being the Church in the Virtual World* (Grand Rapids: Zondervan, 2009), 79.

seventy million people who are active in the virtual world [many of whom are teens]. This means the virtual world is by far the largest unreached people group on planet Earth."[3]

All of this forced me to reconsider my opening gambit. Since I am convinced—radically convinced—that ministry in digital virtual contexts is an essential next step in pastoral and youth ministry, I had to find some way both to attract participants to a workshop on the topic and keep them there and interested for an hour. Even more radically, I would like to build a cohort of ELCA youth leaders who would entertain the possibility of doing cooperative ministry in some of these virtual frontiers.

Hence the "World of Workshop" imaginative meditation I made use of at the beginning of the lecture. If the likelihood of convincing youth leaders to travel to virtual digital worlds is slim, the next best inception I could accomplish is to come game in their real world and make them doubt, at least a bit, whether their reality is as real as they think—even better, to convince them that they are gaming all the time, whether they recognize it or not. Each person inhabits an avatar; actually, people inhabit various avatars; they put on different skins for different virtual worlds, and then they play in those worlds and with those characters. I am not taking the youth leaders to the game. I am bringing the game to them.

If I can convince them of at least this much, then I have brought virtual community out of its cave and into the every day, and perhaps that will mean that by the end of the lecture, my listeners might entertain the (admittedly still foreign notion) that digital virtual worlds are not nearly as far away and strange as they seem, and they are much more everyday than one might think. I will also have equipped the listeners with greater proficiency at appropriating some of the core strengths of the virtual world that can "play" in real-life ministry contexts.

TWO GAMES AND THEIR PROCEDURAL RHETORICAL EFFECTS

In this next section, I will discuss two popular and accessible games. After describing each game briefly, I will draw out one or two key insights into the new culture of learning indicated by these games. Both games are digital, virtual worlds. There are so many games out there that I had to limit this survey, so I followed the rule that I was aiming for massively multiplayer environments that are played by a wide variety of players, games I am personally familiar with, and games people I know personally play. The games will be discussed

3. Ibid., 29.

in approximately the order of age group that plays them. World of Warcraft is more of a high school- and college-age phenomenon, although not exclusively so. Second Life is especially a world of young adults transitioning into middle age.[4]

The busy youth leaders at my lecture would be right to be asking at this point, before they jump in, what the payoff is for them. They are likely wondering why digitally mediated worlds matter. Two short quotes convey the profound significance of exploring this topic. First, danah boyd, an ethnographer in the area of teen networked publics, had this to say in her recent book: today's teens are "the first generation to have to publicly articulate itself, to have to write itself into being as a precondition of social participation."[5] In other words, in addition to what people see teens doing daily in school and church—writing themselves into being through their clothes, music choices, friendship patterns, and so on—they are also doing so in the digital world; and in fact, in their digital networking patterns, that is the *only* way to be there, by writing themselves into being.

The other insight came from Pete Ward, in his book *Participation and Mediation*: "Liquid church expresses the way that ecclesial being is extended and made fluid through mediation. The liquid Church moves beyond the traditional boundaries of congregation and denomination through the use of communication and information technologies."[6] How the church is mediated as new technologies arise is itself a missiological topic. Ward continues, "A central missiological issue for the Western Church relates to how it chooses to react to the mediation of the spiritual in popular culture."[7] Although my profession is as a lead pastor of an ELCA congregation, my tribal identities are deeply tied to youth ministry and mission work. Boyd and others have convinced me that the digital world is increasingly where teens will be, and Ward has convinced me that new mediated forms of pop culture present us with a new missiological challenge.

Finally, a 2008 Pew Internet and American Life study on *Teens, Video Games, and Civics* provides the following statistics:

---

4. Scholars wishing to study an immersive game context especially geared for children should consider, as an alternative, Minecraft.

5. danah boyd, "Taken Out of Context," PhD diss., University of California at Berkeley, 2008, http://www.danah.org/papers/TakenOutOfContext.pdf. (accessed January 16, 2012), 120.

6. Pete Ward, *Participation and Mediation: A Practical Theology for the Liquid Church* (Norwich, UK: SCM, 2008), 137.

7. Ibid., 190.

1. Almost all teens play games. Fully 97 percent of teens ages twelve to seventeen play computer, web, portable, or console games.
2. Youth play many different kinds of video games. Eighty percent of teens play five or more different game genres, and 40 percent play eight or more types of games. Anecdotally, although at the time of the Pew study Madden was the top played game, with Halo a close second, many youth workers I know now report the top games youth play are Call of Duty and World of Warcraft.
3. Gaming is often a social experience for teens. For most teens, gaming is a social activity and a major component of their overall social experience.
4. Playing games with others in person was related to increased civic and political engagement, but playing with others online was not.[8]

WORLD OF WARCRAFT

Some of the high schoolers of my congregation I know primarily through Facebook. Complex family situations preclude them from attending church with any regularity. I receive regular messages, questions, and comments from them, and I would say, without a doubt, that in some cases we know each other well. The ambient intimacy of Facebook as a networked public augments our face-to-face relationships and, in at least a few cases, is the primary relationship itself.

In a couple of particular cases, I have come to know these youth primarily because of their interest in gaming. Some are struggling with various emotional issues. Face-to-face with people, they often feel uncomfortable, even unsafe. Chatting on Facebook or chatting on World of Warcraft (hereafter WoW) is easier. They are literally more open and themselves. For better or worse, increasingly this is true for some youth. Sherry Turkle, in her important nearly fifteen-year exploration of our lives in the digital terrain, recently published as *Alone Together*, writes that many people prefer texting or chatting because in a phone call "'there is a lot less *boundness* to a person.' In a call we can learn too much or say too much, and things could get 'out of control.' A call has insufficient boundaries. . . . When texting, [we] feel a reassuring distance. If things start to go in a direction [we don't] like, we can easily redirect the conversation—or cut it off."[9]

8. Pew Research Center, "Teens, Video Games, and Civics," http://www.pewinternet.org/~/media/Files/Reports/2008/PIP_Teens_Games_and_Civics_Report_FINAL.pdf.pdf, Pew Internet & American Life Project (accessed September 5, 2012).

While I personally do not like texting because it is a less native medium for me than e-mail or chat, I understand this impulse. People like control, even if they feel some guilt admitting that fact. And in fact, past forms of media allowed for similar control over the pattern of communication, letter writing being until recently the preeminent example.

The high school youth with whom I am in relationship through WoW play the game regularly. They noticed that I had been exploring WoW and posting about my discoveries on Facebook. One evening, very late at night, I began messaging back and forth with a few of them about why they play, game mechanics, and preferences for either solo or social gaming. Interestingly, they observed that their communal game play had reduced at the same time as some of their real-life communality had also decreased. Messaging with the pastor was one step back into greater levels of game sociality and real-life sociality.

Generally speaking, as noted in statistics on game play from the Pew study, teens play games with others. This is not necessarily, or even primarily, by playing with others online but can include playing with others in the same room. With increased band-width and improved game functionality, more and more gamers are playing games online with others.[10] Regardless of whether they play remotely online or together in the same room, sharing equipment and consoles, gaming is social.

James Paul Gee, professor of literary studies at Arizona State University and author of *What Video Games Have to Teach Us about Learning and Literacy*, points out the way in which many adults might miss this point via a short story:

> Let me tell you a little story about the social nature of gaming. I don't, in general, encourage baby boomers to rush off and play video games, since the games are often quite hard and can be frustrating for people not willing to confront their own, perhaps rigidified, learning muscles in a new setting. Nonetheless, some older people do run off to play for the first time when they hear me talk (and, indeed, there are a growing number of older gamers these days). One older adult who tried a video game after hearing one of my talks did, indeed, become seriously frustrated. Then his 21-year-old gamer stepson came into the room and asked him, "What are you doing?" The man said, "Trying to learn to play this damn video game." The son said,

9. Sherry Turkle, *Alone Together: Why We Expect More from Technology and Less from Each Other* (New York: Basic Books, 2011), 190.

10. Very popular games, in addition to World of Warcraft, that function in this way include Call of Duty: Modern Warfare, Halo, and Star Wars: The Old Republic.

"For heaven's sake, why would you do that alone?" Ah, so, here is one good learning principle built into gamers, not just games.[11]

This would be a good learning principle to build into churchgoers and youth ministers as well. Youth workers and church leaders would do well not to try and do the hard stuff alone.

After this late-night conversation, I started exploring some of the ways in which games like WoW are themselves intrinsically formative. In the case of WoW, a signature of the game is that players can join together into guilds. In fact, to really succeed in the gaming world and accomplish some of the most complicated quests, and to earn more experience points as a result, the game prefers that players work in guilds, and it sometimes even requires it. Many guilds organize raids with a raiding party of twenty-five players (from around the world) who go on a six- to eight-hour quest to accomplish their goal. In order to succeed at the quest, players also need to do extensive research on the WoW Wikia or use analytic tools to confirm which spells and other items will be most helpful at succeeding. Ultimately, there is also a kind of intrinsic discovery; the group learns together (and sometimes surprises itself) with its success. This raiding culture is deeply and profoundly communal in ways rare even in real-world environments.

My friend A. K. M. Adam, who is professor of New Testament at the University of Aberdeen in England and an avid gamer, took some time to describe to me what he has learned participating in a long-standing guild in WoW. He writes:

> Relative to your specific thesis, I wonder whether there isn't a comparison to be made between the catechumenate and the process of enculturating new members into a MMORPG guild. I mention this because of my experience as a guild admin and class lead (priest, of course) in the very long-standing Warcraft guild We Know whose guild master is Joi Ito, recently named head of the MIT Media Lab. . . . I was at work on the backend, so to speak, trying to help cultivate customs for positive social interaction. Our guild didn't allow racist, sexist, offensive language in guild chat, and regulated group behaviour in a way as grown-up as we could possibly achieve. . . . [Games] tend to bring out the early-adolescent male child in players—and we early on had a lot of trouble with

---

11. James Paul Gee, *What Video Games Have to Teach Us about Learning and Literacy* (Hampshire, UK: Palgrave Macmillan), 2007, 8.

overexcited members. . . . We had to pull people aside, gently and persistently, to say that we just don't talk that way in We Know; that we have members who are gay, who are women, who have children with Down syndrome, who have survived rape. Some people quit the guild, some people groused a lot about "free speech," but by the time I retired two years ago, we hadn't had to rebuke anyone in longer than I can remember. If you joined We Know, you signed up for our way. The longevity, popularity, and success of the guild suggest that something is going right.[12]

Adam focuses on the development of communal norms in a community that is on "a way." There is sensitivity to the real-life situations of those who play the game, but also a sense of what can maintain continuity and commitment in the game itself. This is such a different Christian reaction to the gaming context than is typical in places where leaders are focused around boundaries for game play itself rather than seeing boundaries in game play as being in the service of gaming virtual community.

Gee offers a concise list of what church leaders can learn from gaming and implement in their own teaching and leadership of youth ministry:

1. *Good video games offer players strong identities.* You aren't simply a number or statistic in a confirmation classroom—instead, you are lead hunter or the priest.

2. *They make players think like scientists.* Trial and error are a big part of gaming. Again, this is a nonscientific observation, but I wonder if we allow the same kind of trial and error in our faith formation practices in youth ministry.

3. *They let players be producers, not just consumers.* In a game like Minecraft, for example, the environment is built by the players. In a game like WoW, there is an entire community around the game producing Wikia content and other resources.

4. *They lower the consequences of failure.* If your avatar dies, you can resurrect it and continue the game from that point. Do we let youth fail and build a gaming culture in our churches where the consequences of failure are lowered?

5. *They allow players to customize the game to fit their learning and playing styles.* I even think most youth in our churches think they are allowed to customize the

12. A. K. M. Adam, email interview with the author, December 2011.

church game, even though they regularly customize other domains in which they are participants, and often at an incredibly high level of proficiency.

6. *Because of all the preceding, they feel a real sense of agency, ownership, and control. It's their game.*[13]

This last insight bears special attention. When I talk with gamers, they clearly feel mastery within their domain. They do not need special advice from experts or permission to navigate the world. They are self-engaged, self-directed, and often incredibly skilled. I am learning from them, not the other way around.

This happens because there are systems built into the game itself that build this kind of mastery and confidence. Youth ministries and churches would do well to learn from this. Gee writes:

> Good games offer players a set of challenging problems and then let them practice these until they have routinized their mastery. Then the game throws a new class of problem at the player (sometimes this is called a "boss"), requiring them to rethink their taken-for-granted mastery. In turn, this new mastery is consolidated through repetition (with variation), only to be challenged again. This cycle of consolidation and challenge is the basis of the development of expertise in any domain.

The power of these learning strategies in the game is that they make use of a different kind of rhetoric from church rhetoric, an intrinsic process for learning rather than the typical extrinsic learning strategies so popular in word- or information-based systems. They engage in what is sometimes called procedural rhetoric. Ian Bogost, author of *Persuasive Games*, writes, "Procedural rhetoric encompasses any medium that accomplishes its inscription via processes."[14] One learns the game by playing the game. One learns what the game has to teach by participating in the gaming world rather than reading something about it. One cannot really even comprehend what WoW or Second Life is until one actually inhabits that gaming world for a while, because it accomplishes its inscription via processes. Bogost explains:

13. Gee, *What Video Games Have to Teach Us*, 216.

14. Ian Bogost, *Persuasive Games: The Expressive Power of Video Games* (Cambridge: MIT Press, 2010), 46.

We must recognize the persuasive power and expressive power of procedurality. Processes influence us. They seed changes in our attitudes, which in turn, and over time, change our culture. As players of videogames and other computational artifacts, we should recognize procedural rhetoric as a new way to interrogate our world, to comment on it, to disrupt and challenge it. As creators and players of videogames, we must be conscious of the procedural claims we make, why we make them, and what kind of social fabric we hope to cultivate through the processes we unleash on the world.[15]

SECOND LIFE

I inhabit Second Life (hereafter SL) primarily as a monastic. My avatar, Miroslav Tweedy (Miroslav is one of my favorite Slavic names, and Tweedy is the last name of Jeff, lead singer for Wilco), wears an attractive Roman-style cassock that is a case of completely overdressing for midweek worship. For the early days after my rez date on SL (that is, the day I created my avatar and began "playing"), I wandered the world a bit in order to explore (and in those days dressed like Neo from *The Matrix*). But more recently I have really focused my time there simply praying compline in Christian community, especially with the St. Matthew's-by-the-Sea community, an Episcopal chapel of peace for all people, built in memory of Matthew Shepard and all LGBT victims of violence.[16] I have also participated somewhat regularly in a Bible study hosted by an ELCA pastor (John Stiles) on Thursday evenings and visited worship at the Anglican Cathedral in Second Life and a few other worshipping communities.

Axel Bruns, in his book *Blogs, Wikipedia, Second Life and Beyond: From Production to Produsage*, writes, "Second Life players are engaged in nothing less than the collaborative produsage of the virtual world itself; 'virtually every object, terrain, and animation is the creative work of its membership.'"[17] In some ways, this makes SL less a game and more a multiuser environment. Like the real world, this means SL varies widely from locale to locale, because every place is built out of the creativity and input of users. A few of the possible destinations in SL include: churches; dance clubs; historical reconstructions

15. Ibid., 340.

16. St. Matthew's-by-the-Sea in Second Life, http://stmattsinsl.wordpress.com/ (accessed August 28, 2012).

17. Axel Bruns, *Blogs, Wikipedia, Second Life and Beyond: From Production to Produsage* (New York: Peter Lang, 2008), 298.

of particular eras then available for role playing and game play (westerns, steampunk, etc.); built environments that replicate real life (the Sistine Chapel, downtown Moscow); futuristic universes (Star Wars); reproductions of fictional worlds; universities and businesses that offer classes, advertising, and the like "in world"; and shops where avatars can purchase clothing, furniture, carpets, and much more.

Second Life is the preeminent virtual world for exploring the concept of produsage, because at the same time that folks "in world" are consumers of the SL products, and purchase linden dollars, they are intimately also the producers of the environment on every possible level. Second Life as a virtual world is what it is because of produsage.

There are four core principles of produsage. The first is *openness to user participation*. In many ways, it is dramatically open to user participation in ways that real-life contexts cannot replicate. The second core principle is *communal evaluation*. I have sat after worship some evenings while the worship leader asks us how we should rebuild the chapel. The community gets to evaluate the built space and give input into what everything should look like. The third core principle is that they are *fluid heterarchies*. People come and go from the environment; sometimes they are deeply involved, and later they take a lesser leadership role; and there is a dramatic fluidity to who is in charge and who is participating. Recently, I have seen an increase in this same pattern in real-life congregations. The fourth core principle is that they are *permanently unfinished*. *Prodused* environments are never "done." That is one of their great strengths. These core principles of produsage are absolutely the kind of patterns church leaders would do well to creatively appropriate for ministry contexts, or even figure out how to participate in as ministry itself.

Admittedly, my own participation in SL is probably enabled by my long-standing participation in what one might call sci-fi geek culture. However, there is more to the whole "geek thing" than first meets the eye, and it is this point with which this section will conclude. Increasingly, educational theorists have been recognizing the extent to which the path to geekdom is itself a profound learning culture. Most people who end up geeks start out just *hanging around* in the world in which they eventually geek out. They "rez" in Second Life and go where people are clubbing or dancing just to meet and try out things.

At this point, the central question is: What is one's relationship to others? Eventually, some of those who are *hanging out* start to *mess around*. In addition to attending to relationships in the environment, *messing around* includes beginning to pay attention to the environment itself. For me in SL, this happened when I bought my first clothes for my avatar rather than walking around in the free clothes provided when you first rez in the world. I started to research, at least a little bit, how to buy land and build things. This openness to the environment asks the question, "What am I able to explore?" Finally, when one explores and goes more and more deeply embodied into the world, eventually one day that person wakes up and realizes that he or she is *geeking out*. Douglas Thomas and John Seely Brown, in their book, *A New Culture of Learning: Cultivating the Imagination for a World of Constant Change*, write, "Geeking out involves learning to navigate esoteric domains of knowledge and practice and participating in communities that traffic in these forms of experience."[18] The geek question is: How can I utilize the available resources, both social and technological, for deep exploration?

Youth leaders should be invited to ask what is perhaps *the* intriguing, challenging, and essential question: How can we invite our young people on a journey that results in them becoming church geeks? Since geeking out is so engaging, so playful, and so joyous, it is for this reason above all others that youth leaders need to learn from the virtual world's culture, collectives, and varieties of play.

LEARNING AND PLAY

Play is a disposition, not just engaging with a game. It is an essential strategy for embracing change, rather than a way for growing out of it. Even while developmental psychologists are routinely coming to the conclusion that play-based learning has inarguable benefits compared to other approaches to learning, our culture struggles to actually embrace play. This is unfortunate, because as one might intuit if one sits with the concept of play for a while, openness to play as a way of embracing the world is not dissimilar to ritual and senses of the sacred. By delegitimizing play, or by classifying it as something done only under certain occasions (to relax, to begin a learning session, to do when we are little but not grown up), one fails to embrace it as a disposition. Consequently, one misses out on it as an important resource for faith. Thomas and Brown contend, "Play provides the opportunity to leap, experiment, fail, and continue to play with different outcomes—in other words to riddle one's way through a mystery."[19] Similarly, by discouraging play in social contexts,

18. Douglas Thomas and John Seely Brown, *A New Culture of Learning: Cultivating the Imagination for a World of Constant Change* (New York: Create Space Independent Publishing Platform, 2011), 104.
19. Ibid., 98.

one is at risk of killing rather than harnessing the power of collectives. Thomas and Brown continue, "Any effort to define or direct collectives would destroy the very thing that is unique and innovative about them."[20]

Inasmuch as parents have not encouraged children to play with faith itself, to toy with the divine mysteries, and to do so collectively, with each other and their family and friends, those parents have ill-equipped them to dwell in mystery and paradox. No wonder so many wander away from the faith when they begin to encounter challenges and aporia. They have been offered no playful equipment to gain an epiphany by way of playing with the aporia. People can learn much from the new culture of gaming if they summon the courage to do so.

A Concluding Postscript

One of the most prolific experimenters in the world of game design that enhances reality is Jane McGonigal at the Institute for the Future. In her recent book, *Reality Is Broken*, she writes, "What if we decided to use everything we know about game design to fix what's wrong with reality? What if we started to live our real lives like gamers, lead our real businesses and communities like game designers, and think about solving real-world problems like computer and video game theorists?"[21] McGonigal is particularly interested in exploring not simply how games can be "attractional," inviting people into social gaming worlds where they are challenged and rewarded, but also pushing people out via gaming to be "missional," with games energizing players for engagement in contributing to the world around them.[22] McGonigal has incredibly high hopes—almost messianic in fact—for games and their ability to make people better and change the world. In this sense, she would do well to take into consideration some of the concerns Brock has (outlined in chapter 2) concerning technology as dominant culture. For example, in her book she writes, "This book is designed to . . . build up your ability to enjoy life more, to solve tougher problems, and to lead others in world-changing efforts."[23]

However, as this chapter has discussed, what McGonigal and others are exploring in their work on games is territory that until recently was largely unexplored, so there is also no compelling reason to prematurely rain on the

---

20. Ibid., 54.

21. Jane McGonigal, *Reality Is Broken: Why Games Make Us Better and How They Can Change the World* (New York: Penguin, 2011), 7.

22. Ibid., 10.

23. Ibid., 14.

parade. There are some rather convincing reasons why gaming, if applied correctly, does indeed accomplish things like making people more resilient, happy, and creative. McGonigal recognizes, for example, that "games make us happy because they are hard work we choose for ourselves, and it turns out that almost nothing makes us happier than good, hard work."[24] Games provide a context for choosing hard work (unnecessary work at that), but then McGonigal also notes that this only applies "in game." Many gamers report that (and this is the problem McGonigal is trying to address) they are less happy when not gaming. McGonigal's solution to this dilemma, however, is different from the technological moralists who seek to dissuade gamers from playing. Instead, McGonigal asserts, "we need games that make us happier even when we're not playing."[25]

McGonigal proceeds in the remainder of her book to offer a series of "fixes" for reality she believes games offer. Here is where insights into media effect have immense payoff. The medium, an extension of the human, in its observable effects, ferries key insights back to the human qua human as to the ways real life can be improved. Perhaps the most intriguing proposal McGonigal offers, and the one that resonates the most strongly with our preceding chapter on the catechumenate, is her definition and analysis of "alternative reality games" (hereafter ARGs). ARGs are a model for how to integrate game technologies into real-world activities. She writes, "ARGs are designed to make it easier to generate the four intrinsic rewards we crave—more satisfying work, better hope for success, stronger social connectivity, and more meaning—whenever we can't or don't want to be in a virtual environment."[26] To my ear, this sounds exactly like a description of the catechumenate, its goals and function. In other words, the catechumenal process described in chapter 3 is a great church-based exampled of an ARG. In fact, if the catechumenate were given that description, more people might participate in it than when it is publicized as a catechumenal process.

What is unique about McGonigal is that she does not just theorize about games, she actually invents and plays them. She creates, for example, Chore Wars, a life-management ARG that helps manage chores in one's life like a real game; or SuperBetter, a concept ARG that uses social media and networking tools to virally spread new game ideas.[27] McGonigal is clued into media effects in a very deep way and is not distracted by virtual gaming into assuming all

24. Ibid., 28.
25. Ibid., 44.
26. Ibid., 125.
27. Ibid., 142.

games are now virtual games or that the only games that can be used for improving reality are in digital environments. Instead, she understands that games are the technology, the cultural form itself one inhabits, and is seeking to discern how people can "game" every situation in ways that improve real life.

This concluding idea leads to chapter 5, which will examine various social media and more prosaic faith formation contexts, because there are ways in which games can help people "game" those contexts in more inspiring and productive ways.

McGonigal offers a series of criteria for analyzing alternate reality games:

1. *When* and *where* do we need an alternate reality? Which situations and spaces call for it—and when are we better off leaving reality alone?

2. *Who* should we include in our alternate reality games? Besides your close friends and family, who else would we benefit from inviting to play with us?

3. *What* activities should we be adopting as the core mechanics of our alternate reality games? Game design is a structure—goals, restrictions, feedback—but within that structure, we can ask players to do almost anything. What habits should we be encouraging? What actions should we be multiplying? [28]

This set of questions equips people with criteria for making difficult activities more rewarding, building new real-world communities, and helping them adopt the daily habits of happy people, all of which, ostensibly, are goals of faith formation. Thinking back to the two games under review in this chapter, World of Warcraft and Second Life, such games offer space and context for a wide variety of faith-forming and life-enhancing activities. McGonigal's questions offer a heuristic for technology evaluation. Thinking forward to other mediated or real-life contexts, the tools offer resources to "port" lessons between contexts and across platforms. The next chapter will make use of these insights and expand on them while examining a more traditional and widely adopted media platform—Facebook.

---

28. Ibid., 145.

5

_____

More Prosaic Media Forms and Formation

Communication determine[s] "things to which we attend" and...changes in communication will follow changes in "the things to which we attend."

—HAROLD INNIS, *THE BIAS OF COMMUNICATION*

Central to all problems in the church's use of any medium of communication is the hermeneutic question: How particularly does this medium work within the unitary enterprise of human communication.

—ROBERT JENSON, *ESSAYS IN THEOLOGY OF CULTURE*

The previous two chapters on the catechumenate and MMORPGs addressed rather substantive topics. However, because the present chapter engages such an immense area of study (the faith forming implications of digital social media), it is necessary to parcel off a specific and more encompassable portion that will stand in—as a synecdoche—for the whole. The specific focus will be the analysis of the ELCA clergy Facebook group I launched in June of 2011, now with over five thousand active participants, approximately one-third of all clergy in the ELCA.[1] Focusing on a specific community in a specific social media platform will offer the best way "in." In fact, by focusing one's attention on one aspect of a social network, one will improve both how one "attends" to the medium and gain greater clarity into how the medium "works."

As mentioned in the introduction, we do not as of yet have a complete sense of the effects of new media on the present culture and faith formation practices. We are at this stage only observing the effects of the *shift* to the new media. This is an important distinction. Not only are we only observing the effects of shift to new media, we are also observing what it means to shift into a context where everything is in perpetual beta. So we are observing the effects of a shift to new media that are vast because so many of us are transitioning to communication in these contexts, diverse because there are so many and various platforms for social media engagement, and constantly morphing because most of the companies who have designed these social media sites are constantly tweaking and updating them to meet new goals and reach new users.[2]

Take, for example, the Facebook group that will be the focus of this chapter. Facebook is constantly updating its user interface, almost always without consulting its users. The group I administer, the ELCA clergy Facebook group, has since its inception in June of 2011 seen a transition to the "new groups" format, plus a variety of other transitions in group functionality. Many of these changes have been aesthetic, like updates in what is displayed in the banner. Other changes have changed group functionality itself, the most pertinent of which was the decision by Facebook in "new groups" to allow members of groups to "add" new members without those new members needing to approve or accept an invitation into the group.[3] Similarly, it is possible that Facebook might decide to drop groups at some future date altogether, at which point an active community would, by technological fiat, simply cease to exist. In the meantime, while it does exist, it is available for examination concerning the media effects of more prosaic social media forms for faith formation, and so it is to that topic that this chapter now turns.

1. ELCA clergy Facebook group, http://www.facebook.com/groups/elcaclergy (accessed August 28, 2012).

2. As I write this, I am actively communicating via Facebook, Twitter, and Blogger, maintaining a certain level of connectivity on Google and Spotify, and am considering whether to migrate to Pinterest or Foursquare. Facebook has made significant changes to its functionality just in the past week. The rest have updated their interfaces at least once within the past quarter.

3. This is what Clay Shirky has famously called "ridiculously easy group formation," a phrase he repeats throughout chapter 2 of *Here Comes Everybody*. Clay Shirky, *Here Comes Everybody: The Power of Organizing without Organizations* (New York: Penguin, 2008).

The ELCA Clergy Facebook Group

On a Friday afternoon in early June of 2011, I decided (on a whim) to launch a Facebook group for clergy of the ELCA.[4] It takes very little technological savvy to form a group on Facebook. One simply clicks "create group," gives the group a title and brief description, and then adds members to the group. Facebook had just recently designed groups so that members of a group could "add" other members simply by "inviting" friends they wanted to join, and then those "added" members were automatically in the group. This new feature, together with an ongoing interest in networking with other clergy of my denomination, first inspired me to form the group.

I added approximately thirty friends who were ELCA clergy to the group and posted an initial note encouraging my friends to add their own colleagues. Throughout the day, I monitored the growth of the group. Within an hour the group had grown to five hundred members. By late in the day there were more than one thousand members. I was astounded by the rate of growth. This was not the first group I had created on Facebook, but it was the first group that had "gone viral." Already at this point my curiosity was piqued, wondering what aspects of sociality and technology intertwined to energize some groups and maintain their vitality, while other groups, also ostensibly interesting, fail to catalyze. Within a week, the group had exceeded two thousand members, and the group continues to add approximately thirty members weekly. It is difficult to measure exactly what percentage of all ELCA clergy who are on Facebook are in the group, but there are 7,500 clergy currently serving under call in congregations in the ELCA, and there are 5,000 members of the ELCA clergy Facebook group.

Some description of the group is in order. Over time, I have developed a group description (an editable group profile available to all group members and visible to those considering joining the group), which currently reads like this:

> A Facebook group for clergy of the ELCA. Lots of what we do is "talk shop." The group will function as a "centered-set," the center being ELCA clergy but open to other rostered leaders, retirees, seminarians, etc.

Like the Book of Face itself, the group is in perpetual beta. Plumb-lines for participation: Seek to post reflections that are substantive and pertinent.

Second, it may help to understand what this group "is." It's a closed group in the sense that you have to be added to it or add someone to it (that's just how

4. See the ELCA website, www.elca.org (accessed July 12, 2012).

Facebook works), not everyone in the world can read the content. But since there are over 4900 group members, anything you post here can be read by that entire group, and that entire group can potentially share that information, well … anywhere. It is probably wise to think of content you post here as being similar to what you write for a blog or the church newsletter rather than a private e-mail correspondence or small group conversation.

Third, let's keep the conversation upbuilding in nature. If you have something critical or more difficult to say, consider sending it as a message, but first of all consider whether you really need to say it at all. Does it build up the body of Christ? Ask that question before you post or send it.

Fourth, let's contribute in such a way that we participate in God's mission in the world, and build up and strengthen our church, the ELCA. I for one am proud to be a pastor in this denomination, and hope to see it thrive, grow, creating disciples participating in God's mission.

Fifth, do not post anything on here concerning an individual parishioner or case that is confidential in nature, even if you keep the names to yourself. There's simply too much possibility of betrayal of confidence given the size of the group.

Sixth, please no political campaigning or selling of products. Also, no voting people off the island.

If you would like to refer a thread to a previous discussion, go to that discussion, click on the "time stamp" at the bottom of the post, click on it, and this will provide you with a permalink in your browser search window that you can copy-paste into the thread itself.

The sole admin of the group is Clint Schnekloth. For better or worse, like Fidel Castro, I'm the laissez-faire guardian of conversational "freedom."[5]

That group description describes the ground rules. It may not, however, provide an adequate description of what happens in the group day to day. On a daily basis, this is how the group functions. Members of the group post comments, questions, essays, poems, links to articles, links to blogs, and more. These posts become "threads" when others comment on them. It is not uncommon for a single original post to evoke one hundred or more comments. Whenever a post has a new comment, it jumps to the top of the pile, so the design of the group itself energizes conversation (typically) around the posts that interest the group the most. Over time, most posts drift further and further down and recede from attention as new posts and conversations take their place. For example, on one day, July 5, 2012, new topics in the group include

5. ELCA clergy Facebook group, http://www.facebook.com/groups/elcaclergy/permalink/519005591459649/ (accessed September 5, 2012).

an article about the "Religious Coalition for Reproductive Choice," a proposal for using the word *apostolic* instead of *missional*, a question about what to do with old commemorative church plates, a discussion of my recent article at the *Journal of Lutheran Ethics* on missional ethics,[6] a discussion of best practices for blessing a new prayer chapel, a discussion of whether clergy should attend anniversaries in congregations where they have previously served, a workshop discussion writing the prayers of the church for the upcoming Sunday, and so on.

One of the most humorous posts, and a thread that has remained "live" for well over one year, and in the meantime has garnered tens of thousands comments, asked, "Can someone develop a metric by which we determine the average point at which most posts develop into a sub-thread argument? Then we'll all know how far to read." At first, participants responded seriously to this humorous meta-query about the nature of the discussions themselves, but then over time the thread became a catchall for any kind of discussion or post that did not seem to fit the other more serious and pertinent threads. Energized members continually revive and encourage the conversation. It illustrates, as much as anything in the Facebook group, the collegiality and fellowship that can be sustained in digital social media.

ELCA clergy members are the core participants in this Facebook group. However, as a centered-set group, participants with an interest in ELCA clergy topics also participate.[7] This includes, but is not limited to, seminarians preparing for ordained ministry, missionaries, retirees and clergy currently on leave from call, the CEO of the denominational publishing house, executives in the church denomination, and other rostered leaders in the ELCA. They recognize the group as a place to learn how best to design material for ELCA church ministries, a place to learn about ministry (almost like a free online seminary), and a place to answer questions clergy have about denominational structures, board of pensions, and more. The group includes participants from every synod in the denomination, which means the entirety of the United States is represented geographically, as well as missionaries abroad and clergy serving in denominational locations exterior to the United States. It is a laboratory for the communication of knowledge over time as well as space. Concerning the geographical implications of communication technologies, Innis writes:

---

6. Clint Schnekloth, "What We Believe: Social Issues," *Journal of Lutheran Ethics* (July 2012), http://www.elca.org/What-We-Believe/Social-Issues/Journal-of-Lutheran-Ethics/Issues/July-2012/The-Ethics-of-Missional-Church.aspx (accessed August 28, 2012).

7. A later section of this chapter will return to centered, bounded, and networked sets thinking.

> A medium of communication has an important influence on the dissemination of knowledge over space and over time. . . . According to its characteristics it may be better suited to the dissemination of knowledge over time than over space, particularly if the medium is heavy and durable and not suited to transportation, or to the dissemination of knowledge over space than over time, particularly if the medium is light and easily transported.[8]

A Facebook discussion group is definitely far over on the scale of disseminating knowledge over space. There are no geographical constraints other than access to a device that accesses the Internet and access to an Internet connection node. But Facebook groups may also be unique in that they provide opportunity (if to a lesser degree) of knowledge over time, inasmuch as the conversation threads are diachronic. Clergy return, time and again, to find previous conversations from which they can learn. It allows durable and extended conversations that cross-pollinate clergy groups over very wide geographic areas.

Why Such Energy?

As the ELCA clergy group has grown, I have had cause to analyze why the group has such a sustained level of active participation. Whereas some Facebook groups of which I am a part see little regular activity for weeks, it is rare in this group for an hour to go by with no activity. The interest this group generates is illustrated as well by how much conversation it generates off-line. I regularly receive correspondence from clergy at synodical and churchwide events who are thrilled by the creation of the group. For many clergy, the availability of a "digital ministerium" reduces the isolation they may feel in their ministry setting. Additionally, clergy participating in the group see it as a resource for quick and comprehensive crowd-sourced answers to difficult questions. The group clearly tapped into some kind of communicative need within ELCA clergy that was not being met through other means or media, and once it formed, the generative power of communication within the group became its own attraction.

Participants have reported a variety of reasons for their activity and interest. Perhaps the most prominent is that it feels like the clergy group they have never had—or have seldom had—within close geographical proximity to themselves. For some clergy, this means they live at quite a distance from other ELCA clergy, so a group on Facebook allows connection that transcends geographical

8. Harold Innis, *The Bias of Communication* (University of Toronto Press, 1951), 33.

limitations. For other clergy, although they may live close to other ELCA clergy, they find the local groups difficult, perhaps because local religious politics and competition interfere or busy schedules preclude regular meetings. Therefore, even though they live closer to other clergy geographically, they feel closer to clergy in the Facebook group relationally.

Additionally, there are strengths of the group that cannot be duplicated in smaller clergy groups or synodical gatherings. First, on any given day, participants can post a question and gather wisdom from a very broad cross-section of clergy in the ELCA. Specialized topics still get responses because the group is large enough to include other specialists in that area of study or ministry. The size of the group and energy of the group increases the chance of substantive and lengthy engagement, which has the circular effect of encouraging even more participation.

Second, the medium itself—what might be called "written conversation"—offers space for various kinds of communicators to participate who might not engage the conversation face-to-face. Introverts may take as much time to write a response as they wish. When members go on vacation, they can find the thread that interested them prior to vacation and resurrect it with an additional comment.

Third, there is interest in the group for the same reason so many people find enjoyment in social networks in the first place—it is social. The shared sociality and collegiality is its own kind of reward. If one's day has been lonely, he or she can just log in and discover that "we are in this together." The medium flattens and extends communication in what is otherwise at times a somewhat isolated profession. As social as clergy are professionally, most of that sociality is primarily with their parishioners, not colleagues. If ELCA clergy seek conversation with a community with which they share common religious (denominational) experience, plus all the intellectual and cultural queues that accompany it, there is no larger group in which they can make that happen. The fact that one can glean wisdom and address issues of pastoral theology and ministry is an added bonus.

Alert to Some Dangers

There is much of value in social networking groups, but there are also some intrinsic dangers to the medium worth highlighting. Jacobs's point in his essay in *Shaming the Devil: Essays in Truthtelling* is subtle yet important for this exploration. No one using Facebook groups to build community is doing anything more than creatively implementing a tool designed by someone else. At best they are high-end users of Facebook. Perhaps as the administrator of a rather large group, I might be called a "power user"; but I am not actually tinkering under the hood.[9] The way such a group interacts, its strengths, and the messages it repeatedly conveys are themselves subject to the whims of the designers of Facebook itself. That to which users attend in such a medium is to a considerable extent conditioned by how the site is designed. Users are the coded rather than the coders. Users are self-organizing, but only according to the rules already set up and frequently changed by Facebook itself. Jacobs writes:

> Whatever emancipation or other benefit we receive from computer technology (from any technology) depends on decisions made by people who know how to design computers, other people who know how to build computer components, and still other people who know how to write code. Given the increasingly central role that computers play in our lives, how comfortable are we—and by "we" I mean average computer users—with knowing so little about how these machines came to be what they are, and to do what they do? How content are we simply to roll a mouse across a pad and let someone else's music tickle our ears?[10]

Jacobs was inspired to these reflections by a passage in an essay by Neal Stephenson titled "In the Beginning Was the Command Line." Stephenson writes:

> Contemporary culture is a two-tiered system, like the Morlocks and the Eloi in H. G. Wells's *The Time Machine*, except that it's been turned upside down. In *The Time Machine* the Eloi were an effete upper class, supported by lots of subterranean Morlocks who kept the technological wheels turning. But in our world it's the other way round. The Morlocks are in the minority, and they are running the show, because they understand how everything works. The much more numerous Eloi learn everything they know from being steeped from birth in electronic media directed and controlled by book-reading Morlocks. So many ignorant people could be dangerous if they got pointed in the wrong direction, and so we've evolved a popular culture that is (a) almost unbelievably infectious and (b) neuters every person who gets infected by it, by rendering them unwilling to make judgments and incapable of taking stands.

9. Alan Jacobs, *Shaming the Devil: Essays in Truthtelling* (Grand Rapids: Eerdmans, 2005), 180.
10. Ibid., 175.

> Morlocks, who have the energy and intelligence to comprehend details, go out and master complex subjects . . . so that Eloi can get the gist without having to strain their minds or endure boredom.[11]

Thus, I am an Eloi who receives a bit of acclaim among the Eloi because I have mastered a little bit more of the Morlocks' creation than the average person. In the meantime, the Morlocks toil anonymously at their code and create the conditions under which we Eloi communicate.

It would be a mistake to underestimate the significance of this insight. Increasing numbers of new media critics are attending to it.[12] At root, it is an invitation to consider the implications of the use of specific technology for how we pattern our lives and communication, rather than simply considering how best to *use* the technology. On most days, we just drive our cars. We do not attend to the implications (of which there are multitude) of having access to motorized transportation. The availability of automobiles for our daily lives has all kinds of implications for our friendship patterns, employment, daily schedules, and so on.

However, it is not completely clear whether the knowledge of how to build a car, or even repair its engine, would modify how we use them, or how much impact their availability would have on our daily life choices.[13] It may or may not, depending on many factors. Regardless, it is worth keeping in mind that this whole chapter, and all the insights into community and media that arise from it, are premised on participation in a social network designed by others, and that I, the author of this essay, am myself simply a high-end user of the network, not a programmer of it. Returning to the car metaphor, if I go around driving a race car, I should not be the one lauded for its design. My only glory is in having acquired it (and learned how to drive it).

A recent prescient science fiction novel similarly illustrates the problematic. Cory Doctorow in *Makers* describes two "makers," Lester and Perry, who design a "ride" that is the exact inverse of the more popular Disney-esque

---

11. Neal Stephenson, "In the Beginning Was the Command Line," as quoted in Jacobs, *Shaming the Devil*, 176.

12. In addition to Neal Stephenson's original clarion call, "In the Beginning Was the Command Line," see, for example, Douglas Brushkoff's *Program or Be Programmed: Ten Commands for a Digital Age* (Berkeley, CA: Soft Skull, 2010), and Eli Pariser's *The Filter Bubble: What the Internet Is Hiding from You* (New York: Penguin, 2005).

13. It is possible that they might. Some diesel engines can be modified, for example, to use common cooking oil as a fuel source. Those who learn how to adapt their vehicles for this fuel also find themselves making social connections with restaurant owners and searching back alleys for cast-off oil. Thus, knowledge of the technology also modifies cultural practice.

amusement park rides.[14] Their ride is modified over time by the subtle input of participants on the ride. The ride itself is a series of cabinets of curiosities put together by ordinary people. Those who go on the ride navigate through the installations they are especially attracted to, and these installations change subtly through the interaction of those traversing the space (robots that print 3-D continually create new material and repurpose old material). The ride is an amazing and completely original artifact, so over time word gets out and more and more people come to view it. They even design a networked computer system that allows the ride to exist in multiple geographical locations simultaneously and be modified by the interaction of all users everywhere. Over time a "narrative" emerges in the ride, a narrative that seems to arise out of the collective unconscious of the riders. In other words, by riding, the ride becomes what the riders create. By comparison, traditional rides like those in Disneyland and elsewhere rely on the riders adapting themselves to the narrative already for sale and told by the creators of the ride.[15] In both cases, the coders code the rides, but Perry and Lester code a ride that allows the users to become co-coders as well.[16]

The ELCA clergy group is somewhat more like this "ride" than it is like a monolithic coded space that dictates the interactions of the users. Over time the group has even to a degree developed a narrative, a story it tells itself about itself, and this story makes its way out to other environments where it is attractive enough that new clergy come into the group or even join Facebook for the first time in order to participate in the group. As soon as they are in the group, they are as free as anyone to make the group what it is by what they write and post. The content of the group is "produced" by users rather than consumers.

The Missionality of Clergy Sharing Wisdom

What truly keeps participants coming back for further conversation—the added bonus—is the opportunity to glean shared wisdom in a strong network of weak links. The group, because it is broad-based, begins to think of itself as a church of the whole rather than simply one parochial part of it. It is a group of thousands of weak links, inasmuch as every member of the group is a member of the group but may not have any other stronger connection (strong links might include, in this context, serving churches geographically close to each

14. Cory Doctorow, *Makers* (New York: Tor, 2010).

15. This is what we might call "geek" or "fan" culture.

16. This is what Henry Jenkins calls "produsage." See Henry Jenkins, *Convergence Culture: Where Old and New Media Collide* (New York: New York University Press, 2006), 25.

other, or the link between a pastor and his or her bishop, an assistant pastor and his or her senior pastor, and so on). By hosting many weak links, the network as a whole is strong, and this strength is also that which benefits the group and energizes it. So the type of network the group *is* affects how precisely the group *forms*. Participation in the ELCA clergy Facebook group has the double effect of resourcing clergy in a new and innovative manner, but then it also "mods" (that is, modifies) that to which those who participate in it attend because of the nature of the connections they make as they participate. Because it is a scale-free network, with certain participants themselves serving as rich connectional nodes, while other participants are more isolated, it becomes a network that opens up connections in new and unique ways. The group serves as an online ongoing catechumenate for clergy, and as observed in previous chapters on the catechumenate and MMORPGs, media effects matter for precisely what kind of faith is being formed and how.

One intriguing manifestation of this form of networking is how the network makes space for missional engagement in weak and often nonintentional ways. Small groups will spin off from the main group to study a book together or discuss a topic of interest to that small group but not the whole—but the individual participants of that smaller group would not have found connections on that topic if it were not for the existence of the group as a whole. Similarly, next year some clergy from the group will go on a cruise together, and have invited a professor from Luther Seminary to host a continuing education event on the cruise regarding "Preaching Towards Lent." That strong, real-body event could only be pulled together by a weak but expansive set of connections.

However, even these results, that new groups are formed by way of the larger group, do not yet pinpoint the deepest missiological insight. In addition,

> the network understanding of the strength of weak links is very freeing for intentional missional engagement. Embracing the strength of weak links frees you from feeling the need to "fix" or convert the other, from the feeling that you must solve a problem, while simultaneously linking two formally disparate clusters together to move in the direction of mutual transformation. The strength of the weak link is that a new relationship is now formed between two people who are each webbed together in at least two different clusters. These two clusters now cross-pollinate. Both begin to be transformed by the encounter.[17]

In this perspective, connections are not to be pursued for utilitarian ends, but are an end in themselves, because the result of new connections is cross-pollination that results in transformation precisely out of the new connection that is made between the two or more parties. In an early essay on "Church and Electronic Mass Media," Robert Jenson intimates this even as he operates out of some residual utilitarian assumptions:

> One thing we can do over the mass media is thus to educate about the faith. And here the possible internal and external uses of the media merge; we can, perhaps without too much distinction, use them to educate both our own scattered flock and the world out there, insofar as the world has any curiosity about the phenomenon called Christianity. There is a second thing the church can do over the mass media: we can present not the gospel but ourselves as the people of the gospel, for better or worse. We can use the media as permission for the world to spy on us—much as the windows which St. Peter's Church opens onto Lexington Avenue in Manhattan draw a constant group of liturgy observers, some of whom later come in to participate.[18]

Although Jenson may not use the word, he is discussing precisely the way in which mass media can be "missional." As Dwight Friesen points out in *Thy Kingdom Connected*, "The first practice of missional linking is what Paul is most known for: intentionally seeking to be in relation with the 'other.'"[19] A Facebook clergy group allows thousands of ELCA clergy to "spy" on each other, and then, in addition, comment and so be in relationship with the "other."

This is limited otherness, inasmuch as an ELCA clergy group is by nature more of a close, differentiated community than it is an open system, but this is actually a strength for open missionality rather than a weakness. Darrel Guder, in his seminal work on missional church, writes, "Connectional structures

17. Dwight Friesen, *Thy Kingdom Connected: What the Church Can Learn from Facebook, the Internet, and Other Networks* (Grand Rapids: Baker, 2009), 139.

18. Robert Jenson, *Essays in Theology of Culture* (Grand Rapids: Eerdmans, 1995), 162. Jenson tends to say that one cannot proclaim the gospel per se through mass media, an assertion that I question and take issue with. For example, he concludes his essay by writing, "By mass electronic media, we cannot speak the church's primary message, both because the media are mass and because they are electronic. But we can teach theology and we can invite the world's observation. That is very much, and is surely enough to keep us busy." Jenson, *Essays in Theology of Culture*, 162.

19. Friesen, *Thy Kingdom Connected*, 137.

are missiologically essential to the apostolicity, catholicity, holiness and unity of the church. . . . The movement toward missional connectedness should be centrifugal, starting from participating communities and expanding to the global dimensions of the church."[20] A community needs a center if it is ever going to be anything for others. There needs to be a "there" there. For example, early in the formation of the ELCA clergy group, discussions of how open or closed the group ought to be predominated. Some members wanted to rename it just an "ELCA" group and open it up to all participants. Others were concerned that calling it a clergy group, though somewhat appropriate, would exclude others who were "like" clergy but not exactly clergy—such as leaders rostered in other ecclesial systems in our denomination (bishops, professors, deacons, seminarians, etc.). In the end, the community had to perform a delicate dance of maintaining a clear identity, functioning as a close, differentiated community rather than a completely porous one. Friesen also writes, "How do we foster the ecosystem of our faith communities so that they are organizationally closed, thus creating a *We* identity, while ensuring that they are structurally open so they are being transformed through encountering other people, ideas, cultures, and experiences?"[21]

This question Friesen poses is perhaps the key missional question to ask of any community, and so it is a question I continually ask myself as administrator of the ELCA clergy Facebook group. It is not the kind of question one resolves, and then implements the answer as a strategic plan. Rather, it is the kind of question any group needs to perpetually ask of itself in order to maintain its "we" identity while remaining structurally open to the other. Such questions are the engine that maintains group vitality. They are missiological rather than utilitarian inasmuch as they are asking, "How shall we keep doing this?" rather than "towards what final end are we doing this, and what will it accomplish?" A series of theses are offered here in conclusion, all of which offer examples of how maintaining this creative tension in practice opens out the conversation in social media so that the *how* of the medium serves the continuing formative nature of it.

First, groups like this are difficult to "mobilize," but when they are mobilized, they are powerful. My most unsuccessful attempts to moderate the ELCA clergy Facebook group have been when I tried to "mobilize" the group for collective action. One early attempt was to take up a collection for the Lutheran church in Joplin, Missouri, that was destroyed by a tornado that

20. Darrel Guder, *Missional Church: A Vision for the Sending of the Church in North America* (Grand Rapids: Eerdmans, 1998), 264–65.

21. Friesen, *Thy Kingdom Connected*, 153.

ripped through Joplin in 2011. Although many pastors in the group (and the many congregations they represented) were indeed taking up collections for disaster relief, the group as a whole, as the Facebook group, saw little need for (and in fact saw problems with) a collection that came specifically from the group. So members posted comments resisting the idea, and ultimately it fizzled. The group has a kind of "Don't mess with us" mentality, inasmuch as the group does what it does, and if the group as a whole ever feels herded in a specific direction or toward a specific cause, this goes against the overall sensibility of what the group is and how it functions.

That being said, it is fairly clear, given how large the group is, that if the group did self-organize around a common goal, it would have an incredible impact on the life of our denomination. Leonard Sweet, in his book, *Viral: How Social Networking Is Posed to Ignite Revival*, writes:

> For the first time in history, the majority of humanity is connected. In a world of hyperconnectivity, when three-quarters of humanity may be connected by mobile communications by the time you read these words (2012 or later), the amplification of resources and capabilities is exponential. In the words of Australian futurist Mark Pesce, "Hyperconnectivity begets hypermimesis begets hyperempowerment." Or in more accessible language, "After the arms race comes the war."[22]

The point here is that the ELCA clergy group could become one of those "ridiculously easy group" movements if it could decide what to move on, but it seems fairly clear that the group is often resistant to, or at least disinterested in, group movement or action in any traditional sense of that term. Nevertheless, I remain curious about the possibilities of mobilization.

Second, the way groups talk to each other internally matters both for the "we" and for the "other." An intriguing aspect of the ELCA clergy group has been that it is less "attack" oriented than other previous discussion groups online. This is much discussed in the group. Even a small amount of argumentation or flaming at each other is typically frowned upon, and discussed, but overall participants notice that the amount of egregious negative rhetoric is tempered compared to other groups. For Sweet, this is a result of the transition from a Gutenberg (book-based) to a Google (web-based) culture. He writes, "The TGiF [Twitter, Google, iPad, Facebook] culture, at least as

22. Leonard Sweet, *Viral: How Social Networking Is Poised to Ignite Revival* (Colorado Springs: WaterBrook, 2012), 162–63.

it is captured in Facebook, is in favor of 'liking' something. It has no built-in template for 'disliking.' Facebook is on record as being against against. It has said no to negativity."[23]

Third, there is considerable inventive and entrepreneurial opportunity in the bringing together of opposites. One of Sweet's central theories in his book *Viral* is that the new culture is one that embraces paradox. He writes, "Whitehead was right in his thought but wrong in his valuation of what that 'invention' [in the nineteenth century] was, which he thought was organized research and development. The real method of invention is the bringing together of opposites."[24] Sweet continues, "Social networks such as Facebook help to trigger creativity mash-ups by randomizing our lives so that conceptual collisions can occur. TGiF culture is generative because it is constantly jarring us with the introduction of contradictions, oppositions, and exposure to unrelated concepts."[25] This seems true, although a more sustained argument would need to be made that these digital social networks create jarring mash-ups with greater frequency than other kinds of social networks prior to the digital era. His argument, though attractive, may also be somewhat overstated. What the quote does, however, is highlight one opportunity intrinsic to communication in a social network—if one pays attention, and if one attends with an open mind to the jarring incongruities of what flows past one's Facebook feed, rather than filtering and organizing according to taste or interest, one can benefit from the frequency and quirkiness of the mixing of unrelated concepts.

Fourth, networking *is* information sharing. Social networks are social search engines: Alexander Halavais, in his book, *Search Engine Society*, writes, "One of the most natural ways of making use of [a] network is to find information. As we have seen, there is a good chance that someone affiliated with you is more likely to be able to provide relevant referrals. By mining our social networks, we provide some basis for finding and evaluating resources."[26] Membership in a responsive and extensive group is formative precisely because of the information sharing that can occur within it. Since a good deal of *formation* has to do with access to *information*, this is an often unremarked but important consideration.

Fifth, the maintenance of "we" in the presence of "others" invites members to consider their own identity and digital footprint. Here is an example of a

23. Ibid., 171.
24. Ibid., 170.
25. Ibid., 171.
26. Alexander Halavais, *Search Engine Society* (Cambridge, MA: Polity, 2009), 172.

message I received by private messaging on Facebook from a member of the ELCA clergy group:

> Greetings, Clint. I know the Clergy group has been awash with the topic of "privacy/public" nature of things within the "closed group." This is not to re-hash that, but I'm finding myself inhibited to post some things, now that I am actually in a call, and several local colleagues are members. I WANT to trust, but while I was in seminary, I became keenly aware and sensitive of sharing things within collegial groups exactly because of how things got around. I'm reaching out to you, an experienced pastor and e-media user for some advice on whether to heed my inhibitions and participate in only the mundane conversations or to "damn the torpedoes" and see what happens. I would welcome and appreciate any insight and wisdom you'd care to share.[27]

Here was my response:

> I think each person develops their own comfort level on this. I've taken the "wide open" approach. I am who I am in social media, take it or leave it. Of course, my filter is, I try as much as possible to be honest and faithful in whatever I post. Sometimes I fail. Then I ask for forgiveness. But I don't worry what my area clergy think of what I might post in the group. That's my own practice, blessings as you discern yours.

Like much of life, there are not settled answers for how to proceed. Instead, two people make use of their own personalities and patterns to engage in a dialogue that assists in developing an approach. Together the two of us are discerning how to "write ourselves into existence" in the digital world we are ever more frequently inhabiting, and we are doing this with one ear tuned to the "we," and the other ear tuned to the "other."

Sixth, social networking *is* spiritual. One of the continuing struggles in our transition to a fully digital age is to acknowledge that the new media is not secondary commentary on previous media, but is itself a medium in its own right. So, many Christians and church leaders probably think you can make use of social media to enhance or supplement ministry. But it is a fundamental

---

27. Anonymous member of the ELCA clergy Facebook group, email message to the author, July 1, 2012.

category shift when ministers begin to think of social media *as* ministry. Much the same can be said about social networking and spirituality. Rather than looking at Facebook or other media as resources that can enhance spiritual life that happens elsewhere than here, we can invite ourselves to consider the ways in which participation in Facebook and Facebook group is itself spiritual. This is illustrated nowhere more concisely than in a recent response from a friend to a question I had posted about Facebook as a faith formation resource, who wrote, "I have adapted my habit of praying with someone when they ask me to pray for them to type a prayer and post it to their wall." It is simple yet profound transitions such as this that are the hallmark of the transition currently occurring in the trans-media era. Similarly, and as a personal anecdote, although I no longer participate in a local clergy pericope study group, I am a member of a Facebook pericope study group that emerged as an offshoot of the ELCA clergy group. In many ways, I value the conversation in this group as much as I did face-to-face discussions in previous groups of which I was a participant. In this sense, Facebook has not layered but supplanted my previous formative habits.

Many of the media effects analyzed in this chapter continue to expand the sense in which media effects are in themselves faith forming. Although not strictly games or catechumenal, social media platforms like Facebook offer contexts for formative activities with close resonances to the mediated environments described in preceding chapters. It is now time to turn our attention specifically to the theological dimensions of all this formation and media participation. Although hopefully readers have been able to creatively discern the ecclesial or pneumatological dimensions intrinsic to our discussions in these chapters (and perhaps have even learned to think with greater subtlety about the sometimes false distinction between secular and sacred), it is nevertheless worth our time to reflect on faith formation in a trans-media culture in its Trinitarian and theological dimensions.

PART III

Inspired Mediation

6

On Pneumatology and Material Culture

Rather than locate mediation within ideas of omnipresence or in a theology of creation, the relational and personal presence of God might be seen as 'epiphany.' Epiphany emphasizes revealing moments. In epiphany God is intentionally and personally present in mediation.

–PETE WARD, *PARTICIPATION AND MEDIATION: A PRACTICAL THEOLOGY FOR THE LIQUID CHURCH*

At this point in the book, I am tempted to claim that in the final theological analysis, everything that has gone before, even those topics that have appeared completely secular, sociological, ethnographic, cultural, or technological are in fact spiritual. No special theological discourse transcending or layering over the previous discourses is necessary. In fact, such a discourse on the theological or spiritual analysis of media and faith formation would itself be problematic because it reinforces and reifies a dichotomy between the secular and sacred. So this chapter could be very short. It might read something like this: "Christ works through faith formation technologies. God is in the gears. Social media is spiritual. MMORPGs are a proleptic taste of the New Jerusalem. God as Trinity is into new media and especially likes the catechumenate."

I write this somewhat in jest, and yet such claims have merit. Often one looks for the activity of God, the work of the Spirit, and the presence of Christ in all kinds of places separate from the very places one tends to hang out. It is difficult to believe that God can be "here," wherever one may be, perhaps on a futon typing words on an old Mac laptop. Yet the answer is God is there and can be there. Perhaps God is nowhere else. However, a theological analysis is still necessary, because although it is certainly true that God works through means, God seems to have preferred means for working God's work in the world. It is important, then, given this reality, to try and tease out precisely what aspects of the development of new media are especially fertile for the Spirit, which aspects of new media are in actuality more of an obfuscating attraction rather than a mediating material reality.[1] Much of the contemporary discourse around technology tends to either demonize or deify it; in this situation, subtle awareness of theological implications is as important as the awareness of media effects we have been trying to cultivate in previous chapters. A common thread has been emerging in all the chapters leading up to this one. In various ways we have been illustrating that faith formation and material culture are inextricably linked, even inseparable. Examples abound. Formation of preachers as proclaimers of the gospel is directly connected to, embedded in, how their brains are hardwired and continually forming neurologically. Humans, though they speak of technology as if it were separate from them, are virtually incapable of living a nontechnological existence.[2] New media, video games, and social networking are all mediated through digital means. In fact, nothing of contemporary life is unmediated. Even procedures, habits, and actions are themselves technologies, or media, as are various kinds of procedural rhetoric. Pete Ward notes, "The communication of the Church operates as a series of mediations. Mediation therefore presents as culture, but it is also a participation in the Trinitarian life of God."[3]

1. In *Power Failure*, Albert Borgmann writes, "Fundamental theology today must be a theology of technology, the successor to medieval natural theology. By a different path the student of technology may also be led to something like theology." Albert Borgmann, *Power Failure: Christianity in the Culture of Technology* (Grand Rapids: Brazos, 2003), 81.

2. See A. K. M. Adam's thought experiment into a life completely free of technology in "The Question Concerning Technology and Religion," http://www.elca.org/What-We-Believe/Social-Issues/Journal-of-Lutheran-Ethics/Issues/November-2012/The-Question-Concerning-Technology-and-Religion.aspx. Adam writes, "In order to get a perspective on the relation of technology to religion, we ought perhaps to begin by trying to imagine religion *apart from* technology. In this exercise, we imagine a worshipper apart from walls and edifices, encountering the divine without mediation by any human products. To complete the worshipper's isolation from technology, we will remove not only portable electronics, eyeglasses, watches and jewelry, but also any manufactured clothing. We will still not have attained pure isolation—our worshipper has been immersed in technological devices all through life—so our hypothetical worshipper must spend a prolonged interval naked in the wilderness, so as to lose some of the habits of living in a technologically-defined culture. After subsisting apart from all constructed devices for several weeks, shedding as much as possible the influences of reliance on technology, one might come optimally close to purging the residual effects of technology from one's confrontation with God."

THE GHOST IN THE GEARS

To raise awareness of theological implications, a rather remarkable and famous essay by Walter Benjamin, "The Work of Art in the Age of Its Technological Reproducibility," provides a start. Here is an excellent test case, because at first look, it seems referencing Benjamin's work is simply once again attending to secular cultural analysis rather than the theological canon proper. However, Benjamin begins his essay arguing that the work of art prior to the age of technological reproducibility had an "aura" because it had a history and was embedded within a tradition. This "aura," he explains, is "a strange tissue of space and time: the unique apparition of distance, however near it may be."[4] This aura is familiar to us today; it is the awe experienced because of the proximate distance from us of a celebrity, a historic painting, or architectural wonders. Benjamin, however, sees strange things happening to this aura in the era of mechanical reproducibility, arising out of "the desire of the present-day masses to 'get closer' to things, and their equally passionate concern for overcoming each thing's uniqueness by assimilating it as a reproduction."[5] Already at this point it is clear that careful cultural analysis on Benjamin's part is bearing theological fruit. Then he continues:

> The stripping of the veil from the object, the destruction of the aura, is the signature of a perception whose "sense for all that is the same in the world" has so increased that, by means of reproduction, it extracts sameness even from what is unique. Thus is manifested in the field of perception what in the theoretical sphere is noticeable in the increasing significance of statistics. The alignment of reality with the masses and of the masses with reality is a process of immeasurable importance for both thinking and perception.[6]

Benjamin's insight here is remarkable. He turns the tables on statistics. Instead of statistics serving as a secular science that can inform ecclesial discourse, Benjamin sees the rise in significance of statistics occurring precisely as the result of an apocalyptic flattening, even dissolving, of reality into the masses and the masses into reality. Statistics are the new religion. At the very least, this is a theologically anthropological observation. It may even have soteriological

3. Ward, *Participation and Mediation*, 111.
4. Walter Benjamin, *The Work of Art in the Age of Mechanical Reproducibility and Other Writings on Media* (Cambridge, MA: Belknap, 2008), 23.
5. Ibid., 23.
6. Ibid., 23–24.

implications. Aura is transfigured and displaced in this new era, and just so what is perceived as spiritual and real are perceived differently because of the rise of new (reproducible) media. More precisely, in the case of statistics, which are a perfect example because statistics are so often referenced in ecclesial strategies and planning, statistics become not tools for "reading the audience" but are instead what make reality itself and become the new scripture. Statistics in this picture do not simply give us new insight into reality. Instead, statistics *are* the reality to which reality then conforms. In short order, the degree to which cultural analysis properly considered is itself theological has already been illustrated.

Theologians working not out of cultural analysis like Benjamin but out of their own fields of missiology and theology often come to similar conclusions. For example, Ward argues that "culture as a category opens the field for a less alienating kind of theology."[7] In some forms of traditional (and especially modernist) theology, theology is abstracted from daily practice and stands apart. Ward notes that increasingly theologians have been finding that approach to theology unsustainable and have been making a turn to the cultural. Ward continues, "The significance of the cultural is that it not only serves to locate theological work as a conversation concerning the practice and expression of the Church, but it also identifies the activity of the theologian as itself a form of practice."[8] Even theology itself, in this view, is cultural, mediated, and material. The one form of discourse remaining one might have thought could stand aloof from the material world is itself material and is more spiritual precisely when it recognizes its own status as a practice in culture.

Discerning the Spirits

This chapter then proceeds in identifying the pneumatological dimensions of material culture, especially aspects of material culture related to faith formation and media, by noting that in fact all of spiritual life is mediated and all media is potentially pneumatic. This is done quite simply, precisely by being aware of this fact. Awareness of the proper relation between the two is itself the first step. Other steps proceed from this first step.

One example is the catechumenate. The catechumenate is a process, a kind of procedural rhetoric, certainly. In this sense, it is a technology informed by technological thinking. However, it is also a faith-forming process centered on the sacraments. In this sense, the catechumenate is unique in that it is a

---

7. Ward, *Participation and Mediation*, 34.

8. Ibid., 41.

faith formation technology that takes account of its own materiality precisely in its spirituality because of its sacramental and mystagogical components. One might even say that the catechumenate is the *epitome* of mediated spiritually because of its layering around and attention to the sacraments. The catechumenate also epitomizes mediated spirituality, because in and through the catechumenal process, one can see the way in which the theological is not *reduced* to the cultural but is expansively encompassed in it, and vice versa.

An example of this is Albert Borgmann's comparison of the culture of the world and the culture of the table. In his view, "As we move from the culture of technology via the secular culture of the sacred and the divine to the precincts of the sacraments, one thing we need to acquire and bring along is a sense of discipline and excellence when it comes to celebration."[9] This is to say that Christian faith formation in its sacramental dimensions does not transcend technology or move away from it but works within and through it for its own ends and in its own manner, and it does so best when it is theologically aware of itself as a *material* spirituality.[10]

Ward offers one of the more in-depth examinations of one sacrament, the Eucharist, as it pertains to mediation. He examines the mediation of communion under a threefold rubric of production, representation, and consumption. In each of these stages, he carefully identifies how culture and theology overlay each other in sacramental practice, but then he repeatedly argues that such considerations do not "necessarily entail the reduction of the theological to the cultural."[11] This is so because Ward takes an expansive rather than reductive approach to the interrelation of cultural and theological analysis. His concluding statement is worth quoting in full:

> In the Eucharist theology is animated and set in motion as a lived-in culture. It is therefore an embodied "theology." This cultural reading of the theological, however, also implies that it is simultaneously a place of spiritual significance and experience. The performance of

---

9. Borgmann, *Power Failure,* 127.

10. "One of the first things that should strike us about Christian worship is how earthy, material, and mundane it is. To engage in worship requires a body—with lungs to sing, knees to kneel, legs to stand, arms to raise, eyes to weep, noses to smell, tongues to taste, ears to hear, hands to hold and raise. Christian worship is not the sort of thing that ethereal, disembodied spirits engage in. . . . This liturgical affirmation of materiality is commonly described as a *sacramental* understanding of the world—that the physical, material stuff of creation and embodiment is the means by which God's grace meets us and gets hold of us." James K. A. Smith, *Desiring the Kingdom: Worship, Worldview, and Cultural Formation* (Grand Rapids: Baker Academic, 2009), 139, 141.

11. Ward, *Participation and Mediation,* 127.

the Eucharist mediates divine encounter. This mediation is not an interpretive layer placed over the cultural. The indwelt-ness of the Eucharist is there in the biblical text of the words of institution. It is there in the way that this text has been "produced" through liturgical and theological scholarship. It is there in representation and it is there in the way that individuals and communities make meaning and identity in relation to performance. In performance the discursive practices of the Christian community are seen as being a place of divine participation. In performance individuals and communities are "indwelt." There is then a relationship between the way that representation and discourses are animated in the Christian community and the mediation of the life of God. This is true for the communion services but is also true for theological expression more generally.[12]

So this, at least in part, is what discerning the spirits looks like. Keeping an eye out for the work of the Spirit in trans-media contexts is not like watching for the rare appearance of *muscae volitantes*. The Spirit should not be compared to unusual floaties in the eye that obscure vision and are notable only for being out of place. The Spirit in trans-media, rather, is just so the Spirit of indwelling, the taking up of place precisely in and through mediating cultural forms, always toward the best, the divine, the future, the love. This may in fact be all a sacrament is—a material in and through which, by the mediating power of words, liturgies, and more, the spiritual is encompassed precisely in and through and under rather than around or above the material.

THE SPIRIT IS THE SPIRIT

Finally, there is a consistent danger as new media emerges that communities will respond to the new media with disdain and fail to recognize the pneumatological dimensions of trans-media effects. This is a corollary of a danger highlighted early in this book, that by labeling some media "virtual," it is negatively portrayed because it is less than real (whatever "real" is or signifies). So similarly, trusted and more long-standing technologies or media typically have greater cultural caché; communities are more certain that these tried and true media truly do mediate the presence of the divine, the spiritual. As a test case, one might consider which is more often understood as an important spiritual moment—praying at the bedside of someone who is in the hospital

12. Ibid., 133–34.

or calling that person and praying with him or her over the phone. Then one might shift one more medium forward and consider whether a prayer posted as a status update on Facebook and then read by the patient is on the same level as praying with the individual in person in the room. Here again are the dangers endemic to this situation, where developments in new media and technology evoke a certain level of skepticism.

Borgmann writes, "Most people, when prompted, would agree with mainstream philosophers that the right ethical theory will guide us to the good life and that the crucial moral problem is to discover which theory is correct. But this is half right at best. The factor that most decisively channels the daily course of life is not moral theory but material culture."[13] Much of the modern world has been programmed to assume that theory about something precedes and leads to different practice. We even struggle to identify what it might mean to operate via a completely material theoricity. Similarly, when it comes to spiritual matters and the presence of the Holy Spirit, this modernist training has led us to assume that spiritual things are those things most distanced from materiality—things like contemplative prayer, meditation, and the like.[14]

This leads to an assertion that may seem enigmatic, but one written with the best possible of intentions. The Spirit is the Spirit. Of the members of the Trinity, perhaps the Spirit is consistently the most misunderstood and the most detached from material life, as if the Holy Spirit were just some "spirit." Some spirits are disembodied perhaps. But the Spirit of God is the Spirit of Life, the Spirit that hovered over the waters, ordered creation, inhabits the waters at baptism, is present in the bread and wine of the Eucharist, breathes our spoken prayers, and groans in all of creation for the redemption of the world.

I will illustrate this with one more reference to Ward before also illustrating it via the work of a few systematic theologians on the work of the Spirit. Drawing on the work of Pierre Bourdieu, Ward asks to what extent the church can be compared to a "field of taste." Ward sees flow happening in the church as Bourdieu's formula, "(habitus) (capital) field = practice," plays itself out. He writes, "Theological capital as it flows through mediation operates as a unit of exchange allowing individuals to function. . . . Flow therefore structures the habitus as way of life. Participation in the flow of expression develops a specific theological capital. Capital is internationalized as part of identity formation, and as habitus it becomes a force that shapes Christian living."[15]

13. Borgmann, *Power Failure*, 24.

14. Although in point of fact even these things presumed to be a-material are themselves, in another sense, they are completely cultural and material.

15. Ward, *Participation and Mediation*, 174.

Ward, however, argues that although this is an adequate description of how communities maintain a static identity over time while offering space for flow among individual members of the community, it does not offer a description of how communities (churches) extend their (ecclesial) life out from the self-contained community. For this to happen, Ward argues that there need to be "liquid" structures that exist outside regular ecclesial life and increase its fluidity. He offers as just one example the Taizé community: "Taizé challenges the assumption that theological capital and the Christian habitus are only generated within congregational settings. Those who have visited the community, sung the song, and so on, have shared in what is a more fluid form of ecclesial life."[16]

This is where the Spirit seems to be at work in and through media, technologies, and structures, precisely through extending and making fluid structures in their interrelations. The trans-media era simply heightens the visibility and availability of this phenomenon. Whereas the church has until now primarily understood the mediating power of communication technologies to work and build theological capital within the "field" of the church, in the trans-media era the church suddenly has an "extended ecclesial life," presenting it with a new core missiological challenge for how to react to the mediation of theological expression not just in the subculture of the church but in the popular culture of the world. Perhaps the most obvious example of this in digital social media is that my personal posts about theological insights or upcoming sermons in my Facebook newsfeed are constantly in the mix with all kinds of other popular culture references by most friends and neighbors, many of whom do not share my Christian subculture. In this context, as Ward argues:

> what seems clear is that the mediation of the divine life that has allowed the Christian community to extend and make more fluid its ecclesial being, suggests that such an enterprise may indeed be possible. The clue to the way forward lies in the freedom of God to be present both in the Church and beyond it through participation and mediation. So like a light beckoning us forward the Spirit is inviting us to find a way to "go with the flow" of the liquid Church.[17]

NUMBERS 11: ELDAD AND MEDAD

All of this brings to mind that great moment in the book of Numbers when Moses gathers seventy elders around the tent of meeting and God takes some

16. Ibid., 186.
17. Ibid., 191.

of the spirit that rests on Moses and puts it also on the seventy elders, and they prophesy (Numbers 11:24-25). That all by itself would have been a significant distinguishing moment in their leadership and ministry. However, the text states:

> Two men remained in the camp, one named Eldad, and the other named Medad, and the spirit rested on them; they were among those registered, but they had not gone out to the tent, and so they prophesied in the camp. And a young man ran and told Moses, "Eldad and Medad are prophesying in the camp." And Joshua son of Nun, the assistant of Moses, one of his chosen men, said, "My lord Moses, stop them!" But Moses said to him, "Are you jealous for my sake? Would that all the Lord's people were prophets, and that the Lord would put his spirit on them!" And Moses and the elders of Israel returned to the camp. (Numbers 11:26-30)

Perhaps no better biblical illustration of the pneumatologically inspired "extended ecclesial life" exists, and the response to the event by Moses is especially poignant. Although Moses the leader does not intend, plan, or organize the descent of the Spirit on Eldad and Medad in the camp, when it does happen, he does not envy but celebrates it. Not only that, but then Moses and the elders go back out to the camp, the very place the Spirit has gone ahead of them, bringing prophecy before they even arrive, the very same prophecy they had experienced in and by the tent of meeting. The work of the Spirit in and through new media is often like this. It is continually catching by surprise those already practiced in certain technologies and putting them at risk of begrudging the new ways ecclesial life and mediation are occuring. The Holy Spirit goes ahead, is free, extends mediated life, and much more. Perhaps one might define the special work of the Spirit in all of these ways as "hyper-mediated."

THE SPIRIT EVERYWHERE

The Holy Spirit puts the "is" back in "is." It is about the work of reducing the remainder, of making the in-between the in-between. The work or place of the Spirit in the life of Trinity is often misunderstood precisely because of this itterativeness. Denis Edwards, in *Breath of Life*, similarly writes, "The work of the Spirit *is* communion."[18] Robert Jenson, in *Systematic Theology*, states,

18. Denis Edwards, *Breath of Life: A Theology of the Creator Spirit* (Maryknoll, NY: Orbis, 2004), 95.

"The Spirit . . . is hypostatically what the Father and the Son are in common."[19] Whether this "is"-ness is in terms of identity, ipseity, or isomorphism, nevertheless, it offers, and this in the patristic tradition as well as on both sides of the East-West divide, a kind of self-reflexive definition of the Spirit in spite of assertions to the independence of the Spirit as a "person." As the direct result of these definitions of the Spirit, Edwards can then also conclude that in the final analysis, in agreement with the theology of Yves Congar, the line between ecclesiology and spirituality dissolves in practice. I will return to this point in a few paragraphs.

This kind of incollapsible collapsibility of the Spirit finds expression in all kinds of ways. The classic definition, from Augustine, is the Spirit as the bond of love between the Father and the Son. In his book, *Pneumatology*, Veli-Matti Kärkkäinen writes, "The Spirit shares what the Father and the Son have in common; in other words, the Spirit is the *communio* between them."[20] Much of contemporary pneumatology simply extends this original definition, always as the Spirit that undergirds the interrelationships between things. Wolfhart Pannenberg, a modern systematician, offers a field theory of the Spirit that lays the ground for his theology of creation, which Kärkkäinen summarizes as follows:

> The Son is the mediator of creation. The Spirit is the principle of the immanence of God in creation and the principle of the participation of creation in the divine life. . . . The Spirit is the environmental network or "field" in which and from which creatures live. . . . The Spirit is the "force" that lifts creatures above their environment and orients them toward the future. So the Spirit as force field is the most comprehensive and powerful field in which creatures move.[21]

However, for Pannenberg and many other theologians on the Spirit, this orientation to the Spirit is not an orientation out of the world but more deeply into the world as it is a part of God's future. So, in the words of Pannenberg's contemporary, Jürgen Moltmann, "This means that we shall be redeemed *with* the world, not *from* it. Christian experience of the Spirit does not cut us off from

19. Robert Jenson, *Systematic Theology, Volume One: The Triune God* (Oxford University Press, 2001), 147.

20. Veli-Matti Kärkkäinen, *Pneumatology: The Holy Spirit in Ecumenical, International, and Contextual Perspective* (Grand Rapids: Baker Academic), 47.

21. Ibid., 122.

the world. The more we hope for the world, the deeper our solidarity with its sighing and suffering."[22]

This definition of the Spirit is nowhere more precisely or audaciously defined, claims Robert Jenson, than in Augustine: "Therefore the love which is of God and which is God is specifically the Holy Spirit; by him God's love is diffused in our hearts, and by this love the whole Trinity indwells us."[23] In other words, there is a sense in which the Spirit collapses the relationships on both sides of the God-creation divide. In terms of the Trinity, the Spirit *is* the love or relationship of the Father and the Son. In creation, the Spirit is the mutuality and relational coinherence of creation. It is no wonder that within the explorations of this chapter one might wonder whether there is any spirituality apart from the material creation—ipso facto it is hard in Trinitarian terms to distinguish the Spirit from the Father and Son in their relations.

If in fact the Spirit does things apart from giving itself in the very aspect of what it does, then one might be able to talk about a nonmaterial spirituality. But in the definitions given here, one sees that the Spirit *is* what it gives. Jenson writes, "If the Spirit is truly a personal being, he finally *has* only himself to give; the notion that the Spirit could give gifts of love without giving himself betrays an impersonal conception of Spirit."[24] In other words, not only can one conclude that there is no special spiritual place to get to apart from the material, but also wherever and whatever is spiritual, it is itself in the Spirit as personal presence. Additionally, and here Jenson goes beyond the traditional polarities to offer a distinctively powerful and positive proposal on how precisely to understand the Holy Spirit as person: "It is in that the Spirit is God as the Power of God's *own* and our future and, that is to say, the Power of a future that also for God is not bound by the predictabilities, that the Spirit is a distinct identity of and in God."[25] It is in this sense, Spirit as the free-life-giver, divine future, or being-as-possibility, that the eschatological aspect is offered, which will play a crucial role in the last chapter on trans-media effects. Rather than perceive the rise of new media as a guarantee of either utopia or dystopia, deriving its shape and subsistence from what has gone before in some kind of guaranteed developing trajectory, if Spirit enlivens all aspects of material and mediating culture, then it is a center of repeating action, a continuing place of possibility, similar to what has been already illustrated in this book regarding media effects.

22. Jürgen Moltmann, *The Spirit of Life* (Minneapolis: Fortress, 1992), 89.
23. Robert Jenson, *Systematic Theology*, 148.
24. Ibid., 149.
25. Ibid., 160.

Pneumatology in this sense simply consolidates this eschatological sense we have been repeatedly discovering.

This chapter cannot offer a full-blown pneumatology in relation to faith formation and trans-media effects, but hopefully it has drawn attention to the manner in which culture, technology, and media inhabit Spirit and vice versa. Furthermore, this mutual inhabitation is related precisely to who and what the Spirit actually is. In other words, by attending to the Holy Spirit, one better grasps what all these various mediating technologies are and what they signify. And similarly, by attending to mediating structures and formative technologies, one might better grasp who the Holy Spirit is. Having taken time in this chapter to attend to the expressly theological dimensions of faith formation in the trans-media era, I will now present a final chapter with a fully integrated proposal for how awareness of trans-media effects can increase one's chances of encouraging beauty, sociality, and hope.

7

Beauty, Eschatology, Sociality: The Way Forward

Space is dancingly experienced.
    –R. Schwarz, *The Church*
        Incarnate

Because 'God' is relational event there cannot be any divine blueprint, but rather a constant negotiation of those spatial forms in which life, justice and joy are nurtured.
    –J. T. Gorringe, *A Theology of*
        the Built Environment: Justice,
            Empowerment, Redemption

Trans-media contexts might be considered as "built" environments. In the preceding chapters, I have discussed diverse cultural constructs, including media and technology. Each of these is an extension of human handiwork—but they are so integrally tied in to who we are and how we live and operate that they are often sublimated to the point of functional invisibility. One rarely thinks of speech or clothes as a technology or media—we just use them. This is, at least to a certain extent, true of any media or technology. They are simply part of the built environment.

Often when we think about built environments, we focus on the architecture. The word *build* is used most often in architectural contexts, and certainly architectural space is one aspect of built environments. But information technology specialists talk about building servers and other information "spaces"—and liturgical arts, digital social media, MMORPGs, and catechumenates are all, each in their own ways, "built," inasmuch as they configure and reconfigure space, place, and more. It is not a huge stretch, then, to contemplate the various media environments that have been parsed in previous chapters, each as a built environment.

T. J. Gorringe, in the first book ever written on the theology of built environments, writes, "Christianity brings to all debates about the structures of the world through which we reproduce ourselves—economics, social and criminal justice, but also town planning and building—its understanding of God become flesh, 'whereby and according to which,' as von Balthasar says, they build."[1] Some of these media contexts build platforms that are in many ways experientially comparable to architecturally built environments. So in Second Life, participants navigate through a graphically rendered space. On social media platforms, networks construct or assemble communities of users together in various patterns and shapes, not unlike the way a church might bring all the members together in the sanctuary then break them out into small groups in classrooms or choir lofts. Similarly, the catechumenate functions as a built environment on the procedural level, inasmuch as it moves participants through a process and weaves various programmatic aspects of congregational life together into a faith formative whole. Or to return to the very first medium considered in this book, the brain of a preacher is itself a built environment because the regular preparation for preaching not only charts new neural networks in the brain but constructs an entire scaffold around which the preacher then hangs a weekly sermon prepared for the Sunday gathering.

Furthermore, Gorringe argues:

A Trinitarian theology eliminates any fundamental distinction between sacred and secular. . . . We find in Scripture, classically in the Magnificat, a preference for the everyday, the modest, humble and ordinary, and we cannot but take account of that in reflecting on the built environment. . . . Christianity, I shall claim, is wedded to the little tradition . . . which for the most part comes to us only in scraps, in folk memories, songs, tales, and ballads, in pamphlets crudely written.[2]

1. T. J. Gorringe. *A Theology of the Built Environment: Justice, Empowerment, Redemption* (Cambridge: Cambridge University Press, 2002), 3.
2. Ibid., 8–9.

Such a thesis offers the intriguing possibility that all the little traditions most church congregations are engaged in from week to week—printing bulletins, worshipping in churches hastily constructed with worn carpet and stained glass poured by amateurs, not to mention discussing congregational events in a Facebook group or planning a meal for the next catechumenal session—rather than being inadequate in comparison to what Christianity typically aligns itself with—the "Great Tradition," are then in fact exemplary of Christian faith precisely in their mundanity.

Previous chapters in this dissertation have discussed how one might see the Spirit of God at work in a wide variety of mediated contexts. In various fashions, this dissertation has illustrated how to understand the secular and the sacred as perhaps not as distinct from each other as is often thought, while avoiding collapsing the difference. This move is made most successfully by adhering to solid Trinitarian reflection. Gorringe writes, "It is the task of the doctrine of the Trinity to obviate the danger of eliding God and the world, and therefore falling into idolatry, by insisting on *both* God's presence to the world, *and* God's difference. The doctrine of the Trinity gives us a grammar by which to speak of God."[3]

Perhaps there is here a parallel, in the sense that the doctrine of the Trinity giving a grammar to speak of God is the theological corrolary of media ecology and awareness of media effects giving a grammar to speak of the human. Gorringe continues, and is worth quoting at length:

> Christians in [mediated environments] "have the opportunity to lead and advocate for neglected understandings of [media contexts] and of civil government," but in order to do this they need serious biblical and theological reflection. Wherein Ben Sparks speaks of "the city" here I have placed the built environment as a whole. Nearly half of humankind live in villages and suburbs, and exactly the same goes for them. What I am attempting is not an essay in urban theology, or theology of the city, although some chapters deal primarily with the city, but a theological reflection on the living environment we make for ourselves. [This is not only a Trinitarian grammar, it is simultaneously a sacramental approach to faith and the world.] The word "grace" is not a reference to a "power" or "influence" breaking through at certain key moments but a way of saying that the God who loves in freedom sustains the fabric of daily life, including our own. "Sacraments" signify precisely this. What

---

3. Ibid., 16.

the eucharist signifies is not the existence of a sacred world set over against the profane, requiring its own sacral space and time, but rather the hallowing of the ordinary—of bread, wine, labour and community. Because creation is grace, grace is concrete: it meets us in what Padraic Pearse called "the bulks of ordinary things"—and this of course includes buildings and settlements, the places in which we live and work. The theology of everyday life, therefore, is a theology of grace as a theology of gratuity, of love "for nothing," and of joy in the minutiae of things.[4]

Thus, another apt way to speak of the collapse of the distinction between the secular and the sacred that has been outlined in the preceding chapters can be to speak of the sacramental nature of media and built environments. One can observe various ways in which built environments "hallow the ordinary"; in this way, creation itself is grace.

However, this is not all there is to say about the grace of built environments. Grace is grace because of how it reconfigures much of what we would otherwise take for granted about place and time. Gorringe writes:

Because the older tradition of grace concentrates on the believer and the sacraments, it misses the political sense of the doctrine, a sense on the whole not much remarked by the liberation theology of the late twentieth century. The doctrine of grace, of the gratuitousness of all things, is, however, the most politically far-reaching of all Christian doctrines. If creation is grace, if I am "a debtor to all," then self-evidently life is not there to appropriate the benefits for myself, to hoard things over against others. The only response to grace, as Barth always insisted, is gratitude, which politically means the struggle for social justice. . . . But grace has always retained in common parlance the sense of charm and beauty, and so to recognise grace as our political principle is at the same time to recognise the importance of the experience of love, friendship, art and beauty to the political process.[5]

It is this final insight of Gorringe's that sets the tone for the three conclusions offered here. The point is, there are three primary aspects of awareness of media effects that can inform Christian life in a trans-media context, but in each

4. Ibid., 24, 18.
5. Ibid., 20–21.

case the obvious first step is immediately transfigured into a secondary move that transforms and deepens it. With these three insights as the conclusion, this dissertation offers not a full-fledged proposal for how to, finally, form people of faith in trans-media contexts, but instead it offers modest proposals into an emerging field in which we are mostly still observing the effects of preliminary changes. But precisely these kinds of forays can change the terms of the discussion and so tweak media effects in faithful and humane ways.

Beauty Is Grace Is Social Justice

If we approach faith formational media contexts as built environments, it thus becomes clear that formation in a trans-media culture will thrive where it attends to the *beauty* of what is built. Built environments evoke much of the spirit of what makes a place, a people, an entire culture. They are the outward and visible manifestation of underlying theological and technological commitments. This beauty is not simply surface beauty, like makeup, but is intrinsically grounded in, and flows out to, something larger than itself. This is so precisely for the reasons outlined above, that the beautiful, intrinsically related as it is to grace, will eventuate in social justice.

This assertion will be illustrated with an example from the catechumenal process, a story Hoffman relates in the first chapter of his book, *Faith Forming Faith*. This is a story that virtually speaks for itself, so it is quoted here at length:

> Ask anyone who was in leadership at the time and they will tell you that the congregational forum at which Kathryn gave her testimony was the transformational moment catapulting Phinney Ridge Lutheran Church in Seattle, Washington, into its new and present era of ministry. The forum was organized during Sunday morning adult education time in order to continue a conversation that had begun several months before. The agenda was to consider extending an invitation to the one hundred men and women of Tent City to spend three months encamped on our front lawn, beginning just a few weeks before Christmas.
>
> Tent City is a well-organized long-standing coalition of self-governing homeless people who have banded together for safety, community, and advocacy. They refer to themselves as "houseless," not "homeless." Over the years since their beginnings, the political situation had evolved in such a way that city ordinance permitted Tent City to encamp within the city limits, but only at places where they had been invited, and for no longer than ninety days in any one

spot. So it fell largely to the churches of Seattle to be their advocates and hosts. No other Lutheran congregation in Seattle had ever taken the challenge, and we found ourselves moved into the conversation by the most interesting of voices, the voice of a third grader.

The previous spring, the Wednesday evening Bread for the Journey class had taken a field trip to a neighboring church that was hosting Tent City. The elementary kids and a few parents went for a tour and conversation with those houseless persons in residency at a nearby United Methodist Church. Bread for the Journey is our Wednesday evening pan-generational, choral, worship, educational, and fellowship program. Before the night of our field trip, none of us could have imagined the deepened education and fellowship that would bear fruit among us. Matthew 25:35, *I was a stranger and you welcomed me*, was about to come to life among us, revived by the Holy Spirit's breath. On the way home from our field trip to Tent City, that still, small, third-grade voice went something like this: "Pastor, when can our congregation have Tent City at *our* church?"

There were enough adults including two key staff people within earshot. It was clear to us in this small circle that this was the voice of the Holy Spirit. We couldn't let the idea rest.

Six months later, we were in congregational forum proposing what at first had seemed like the most remote of possibilities. As unlikely as it seemed, the idea of hosting Tent City was gaining momentum and many were beginning to believe that it could actually happen. But welcoming the stranger, as theologically and scripturally sound as it was, also seemed even for a hopeful realist unlikely at best. This was going to be ministry in real life, not in theological theory. We are an upper-middle-class congregation whose ministry includes a childcare center that daily serves seventy children. Our well-manicured block-long property on the summit of Phinney Ridge is one of the few green spaces in the neighborhood. It was hard for even the most imaginative and liberal proponent of the Gospel to escape the hard truth that people living in adjoining million-dollar-view homes would not instantly embrace our invitation to the homeless as a magnificent idea.

So in preparation for the forum and for the certain possibility of well-reasoned and well-intentioned objections *against* hosting Tent City, the staff and leadership had discussed our strategy for addressing opponents: be good listeners, remain non-anxious, offer insights, don't get into a power struggle. Most of all, point to the mandates of Scripture and stay grounded in the treasure of our Lutheran theology—God's unconditional grace for all. We had even gone so far as to rehearse responses to those who might threaten to leave our congregation, should we choose to move ahead and invite our brothers and sisters in Christ who live in Tent City to join us for the holy days of Christmas and into the new year.

But we hadn't prepared ourselves for newly baptized Kathryn.

Kathryn was one of many adults who, over the years since 1994, chose to participate in the annual cycle of preparation for baptism through Phinney Ridge Lutheran's contemporary appropriation of the ancient Christian practice of the Adult Catechumenate. As her comments were about to reveal, Kathryn was baptized by total immersion. Not only had she gone all the way under the waters at the moment of her baptism, but also the waters had totally covered her with a new way of understanding her life, her faith, and her relationship with the body of Christ.

After listening to the conversation at the congregational forum with restrained patience, Kathryn stood in the assembly and took a deep breath. "I can't believe the objections that I'm hearing to this opportunity. I can't believe them because, as I was preparing for my baptism last year, this is what you told me that being a baptized child of God would mean. You told me that to be a disciple of Christ meant to care for those less fortunate. To reach out to those in need. To share God's love with all people. That's what you taught me it means to be a baptized disciple of Jesus."

And then Kathryn said the most amazing thing of all, the thing that none of us had anticipated hearing, nor for which anyone had rehearsed a response. "So if we decide that we can't invite Tent City to be on our front lawn, I will have to leave this congregation. If Tent City can't be here, then I can't either, because what you have taught me about who we are as the people of God and what it means to be one of you will not be true."

The room fell silent. For all intents and purposes, the conversation was over. To be sure, there were still opponents to address and details to be worked out, but in that single moment of testimony, God spoke to us through Kathryn and, as II Corinthians 5:17 promises, the old had passed away and the new had come. In Christ we were made a new creation. The voice of that third-grade child three months prior was now amplified by the voice of a new child of God. Before long the voices of God's people at Phinney Ridge Lutheran Church joined together to reach out and invite yet other community of God's people who happen to live in Tent City to join us in the continuing discovery of what it means to live as people of the resurrected Christ.

Had Phinney Ridge Lutheran Church not been a congregation practicing the Adult Catechumenate, I believe that we would not have been ready to reach out and welcome Tent City. Bringing new people to faith through baptismal preparation has meant much more for us than simply growing the congregation. It has opened our eyes to a new way of being the people of God in a new age with a new paradigm. Forming others in faith has formed us for ministry and outreach. How those two things are irrevocably connected and intertwined is, in large part, the theme of this book. Phinney Ridge is not an extraordinary place. We see ourselves as a typical neighborhood Protestant congregation facing many of the same challenges that affect any other ministry in North America a decade into the new millennium. We do have the additional challenge that not every congregation faces of being located in a liberal, institutionally suspect setting, where less than ten percent of the population claims any formal affiliation with a faith community. Fifteen years ago when we began the practice of forming new Christians for baptismal living, not many congregations believed that their communities of faith were congregations that could benefit from such a ministry. But the creeping tide of secularism, the growing mistrust of institutionalized faith, and the general decline of church across the country all collide to make a process of faith formation a valuable option to consider. Our catechumenal story is the story of how, through the baptismal preparation of new Christians, we as a congregation are formed in faith and strengthened for mission in the world, over and over again.[6]

Everything Hoffman describes about this event in the life of the congregation takes place through very mundane and ordinary congregational events—field trips, classes, church meetings, and neighborhood conversations. However, all of these aspects of congregational life can be organized in haphazard and ugly

6. Paul Hoffman, *Faith Forming Faith: Bringing New Christians to Baptism and Beyond* (Eugene, OR: Wipf and Stock, 2012), 2–4.

ways, or they can be organized in graceful, beautiful ways. The beauty of the catechumenal process eventuates in a procedural rhetorical power that shapes the newly baptized to be the kind of Christians who can articulate their faith in the way Kathryn did, and shapes congregations to live for social justice directly out of the beauty of the catechumenal process that forms them as a congregation. Media that is graceful and beautiful does not simply regard or repeat social justice to others—as if it would be sufficient to simply talk about social justice in the Bible study classes or preach about it Sunday mornings—instead, it actually results in new forms of social justice and rehearses the practice of it.

The catechumenate is particularly vivid as an example perhaps because it represents and is a kind of entire culture. Unlike some media, which are themselves more narrowly construed and require the cultural context in which they are situated to carry some of the weight, the catechumenate is a kind of culture in its own right. As such, it can do what theorist Andy Crouch argues culture is designed to do: "Culture is not just what human beings make of the world; it is not just the way human beings make sense of the world; it is in fact part of the world that every new human being has to make something of."[7] So the catechumenate is not simply what the faithful make of the church or how they make sense of the church, but it is in fact part of the church that every new Christian has to make something of. This means, at least in part, that "it defines the horizons of the possible and the impossible in very concrete, tangible ways."[8] Given the ways in which a specific culture defines the horizons of the possible, clearly, as in the example of Phinney Ridge and Kathryn above, "Culture requires a public: a group of people who have been sufficiently affected by a cultural good that their horizons of possibility and impossibility have in fact been altered, and their own cultural creativity has been spurred, by that good's existence."[9]

THE FUTURE IS THE PRESENT

Second, it is helpful to recall the discussion of technology assessment in chapter 2, lifting up the danger that such an instrumental view of technology prioritizes, perceiving all things in terms of objectifiability, material efficiency, and manipulability. It leaves little if no space for the divine. Utopian views of

7. Andy Crouch, *Culturemaking: Recovering Our Creative Calling* (Downers Grove, IL: InterVarsity, 2008), 25.
8. Ibid., 34.
9. Ibid., 38.

technology assessment work from the past to an idealized future, in the process automatizing and guaranteeing things like progress and outcomes. In Christian faith, on the other hand, one sees the future on the way to those of us in the present, and so believers strive to think through media ecology in the sense that heaven is a place on earth, and not only is the future on the way, but it is already here. So the corrective, offered in chapter 6, is that in Trinitarian perspective new media, built environments, and technology are perceived not as guarantee of either utopian outcomes or dystopian destruction, but rather they are mediating cultures enlivened by the Spirit that serve as centers of repeating action, continuing places of possibility.

The insight of eschatology, that the future is coming to us in Christ rather than the other way around, has implications for how we live here and now, and our imagineering about the future of media and faith formation in the future can shape how we engage these technologies now. In fact, if the church is truly proactive and culturally creative and inventive, we will, like the early church's adaptation of the codex, or the Reformation's use of the printing press, invent or further the very media technologies we think are most likely to strengthen the faith and the life of the church in its formative practices.[10]

Two examples from earlier in the book serve to illustrate the point. Both the ELCA clergy Facebook group (chapter 5) and World of Warcraft (chapter 4) are contexts where a new concept of "place for repeatable action" can be examined. In the case of the ELCA clergy group, members can function in an ongoing discussion that is diachronic rather than synchronic because the message board is durable over time. Unlike a verbal conversation, where words spoken are only available as long as they are recorded or stored in short-term memory, in the group discussion, posts and comments are present in perpetuity. Although there is a weakness in the system, since discussions that have not received recent comments recede deeper and deeper into a stack of posts that is searchable but typically not searched, the strength is in a widely disseminated and available resource for mutual support and conversation between participants. Whereas other types of built environments such as libraries or books also provide diachronic formation resources, they are not nearly as dynamic as a digital social network. One might almost say that the ELCA clergy group is liking a "living book." It is both a text one can refer to again and again, and it is at the same time immediately responsive to questions

10. See Andrew Pettegree, *The Book in the Renaissance* (New Haven, CT: Yale University Press, 2010), for more on the historical comparison between our own trans-media era and the rise of the printing press in that era.

and comments because the "authors" of the "text" are still around and available to edit and continue authoring.

The other example, World of Warcraft, is a bit more complicated but worth attention. A strength of MMORPGs, as was discussed in chapter 4, is that they lower the consequences of failure. Participants can try out situations, experiment, even live dangerously (with their avatar), and if the avatar dies, they can resurrect it and continue the game with no consequences. Like the ELCA clergy group example, there is a darker side to this endless repeatability, inasmuch as it sometimes cultivates a cavalier attitude to the challenge. But most gamers will not wish to die too often because of the delay and because they want to solve the quest, so the lowered consequence of failure serves more as a training resource than a crutch. What it does—and this is its metaphorical equivalent to the understanding of eschatology supported here—is change the relation to time, so that time is no longer limited but capacious. In an MMORPG one has, in a certain sense, all the time in the world.

This serves as a metaphorical rather than actual insight, because although this is true in the game, it is not true in a larger sense. A clock is still ticking (most gamers have to return at some point to the nongaming world), and the game is only available as long as the creator of the game hosts it, as long as the gamer pays the monthly fees, and so forth. However, it points the way toward the approach to time such media can cultivate, which is the sense that because time is coming to us rather than running out, we already live in a time when there is enough time. This presents opportunities for reconceptualizing how leaders are equipped for ministry. Douglas Estes asks, "Can real-world churches use the virtual world to teach their ministry leaders how to deal with crisis and the toughest of situations before they encounter them in the real world? If nothing else, virtual churches could equip people to minister and serve in a more controlled environment than the real world, some day transferring their skills into the real world."[11] Or, one might add, they may simply make use of those same skills in the virtual worlds they are already inhabiting.[12]

---

11. Douglas Estes, *Simchurch: Being the Church in the Virtual World* (Grand Rapids: Zondervan, 2009), 198.

12. Estes recognizes the challenges of relating virtual to real-world ministries. He writes, "How will [virtual churches] do ministries that appear to be impossible (or at a severe disadvantage) in the virtual world—ministries such as social, helps, or missions ministries? Since most of the virtual-ministry world is unexplored territory, it will remain to be seen how these types of ministries will work when they are started by virtual churches. Can virtual churches be real churches without, for example, social ministries? Or will they redefine what it is to be social in the first place?" Ibid., 202–3.

I Am the Network

The greatest outcome thus far of the trans-media era is the flattening that has happened in culture and sociality. Social theorists talk about this flattening in various ways. For example, Clay Shirky's *Here Comes Everybody* examines the results of people being given the tools to organize together without needing traditional organizational structures.[13] Others observe the manner in which social movements are increasingly ground-up phenomena rather than top-down. Or in the case of Henry Jenkins's *Convergence Culture* examined in a previous chapter, the flattening has to do with the shift to consumers driving production in a way that shifts any hierarchical distinction between producer and consumer by mashing them together as "produsers."

Furthermore, in the trans-media era, it is no longer possible to think of oneself primarily as a node or solitary point, nor is it possible for one to think of oneself just as a link between nodes. Instead, trans-media and especially social media invite us to think in the manner of the South African philosophical concept of Ubuntu (brought to wider attention in the theological community by Nelson Mandela), that "I am what I am because of who we all are." This is how one is to think of himself or herself anthropologically if a person is a person through other people. Social media offers imaginative space to consider how faith might be lived and formed in nonhierarchical yet highly connected ways. Dwight Friesen writes:

> Leading connectively busts the myth of control and proactively dethrones hierarchies, daringly linking people and organizations with God's vision of the connective kingdom and surrendering their personal vision for ministry. In more hierarchical models of organizations, knowledge and connections were seen as power and the person with the most was in control. Knowledge and connections were therefore often held tightly by the leader. But leading connectively invites a redefinition of power. Power is very important in living networks, but it is not hoarded; it flows as a relational lubricant.[14]

Awareness of media effects in a trans-media era opens the imagination to the construction of a *bon mot* such as "leading connectively," changing the

13. Clay Shirky, *Here Comes Everybody: The Power of Organizing without Organizations* (New York: Penguin, 2008), 25.

14. Dwight Friesen, *Thy Kingdom Connected: What the Church Can Learn from Facebook, the Internet, and Other Networks* (Grand Rapids: Baker, 2009), 100.

terms of the discourse on leadership from the style of the leader as a solo and individual node to making connection an adverb to modify "leading." The result is a compelling argument for Christian life as really, truly, life *together*. Formation itself is done together rather than alone, in the same way that God as Trinity does life as Trinity together rather than alone. However, it radically reconceptualizes what *together* means and how it functions. Specifically as it pertains to knowledge and power and formation, together is more together than it was before. In his book *Everything Is Miscellaneous: The Power of the New Digital Disorder*, David Weinberger writes, "We can see for ourselves that knowledge isn't in our heads: it is between us. It emerges from public and social thought and it stays there, because social knowing, like the global conversations that give rise to it, is never finished."[15] Books like this often include an acknowledgments section, wherein the author mentions all those who influenced the formation of the book. The flattening of the world and an increasing focus on the connectivity of knowledge simply takes this one step further and turns the book itself into one long acknowledgment.

15. David Weinberger, *Everything Is Miscellaneous: The Power of the New Digital Disorder* (New York: Holt Paperbacks, 2007), 147.

Summary and Conclusion

The outline and content for the previous chapter came together primarily while I was on a run, pushing my son in a jogging stroller in mid-August. More than two years of research led up to this epinephrine-induced epiphany, but it was the midafternoon jog itself that opened up time to ponder and brainstorm the overall structure, and it was my regular habit of making space during runs for such contemplation, thus mapping deep neural structures prepared for such epiphanies, so that all of a sudden, about fifteen minutes into the run, everything started clicking into place. By the time I got back to the house, I had to sit down hurriedly with a pen and paper and try to write out the structure, all the while moistening the white paper with my sweat.

I am well aware of my own capacity to stay addictively tuned in to digital and social networks. Being aware of this addictive tendency has helped me (at least to a degree) to continue to cultivate practices that disconnect, that ensure I am not always "on," or that I am on differently. Douglas Rushkoff, in his book, *Program or Be Programmed: Ten Commands for a Digital Age*, writes:

> Recognizing the biases of the technologies we bring into our lives is really the only way to stay aware of the ways we are changing in order to accommodate them, and to gauge whether we are happy with that arrangement. Rather than accepting each tool's needs as a necessary compromise in our passively technologized lifestyles, we can instead exploit those very same learnings to make ourselves more human.[1]

It is precisely my awareness of media effects that has reinforced my commitment to run regularly, and it is the regular habit of running regularly that offers space for deeper insights into the awareness of media effects for this book. I cannot imagine a better story to tell as a conclusion paired to the introduction, because this once again illustrates the mediating power of various practices. Regular rehearsal of the contents of this book, combined with lots of previous writing and reading, resulted in my brain being prepared to shape and outline an entire chapter's worth of content while out on a run.

---

1. Douglas Rushkoff, *Program or Be Programmed: Ten Commands for a Digital Age* (Berkeley, CA: Soft Skull, 2010), 40.

That is a story about practices and formation. The next and final comment is an observation concerning the writing of dissertations as a formative practice. One way the writing of dissertations differs from the writing of books for publication is that dissertations are often designed as a process to help one attain the skills to do other things. They teach the writer how to write a first book so that he or she can write more books. They enforce certain forms of research and editing that will serve the writer in future academic work. Dissertations are nothing if not a formative practice.

This is a book that originated as a dissertation. It looks primarily to other books (see the extensive bibliography) to find the wisdom and rational argumentation necessary to defend a thesis concerning raising awareness of trans-media effects. This is not without irony. If a dissertation is a faith formation tool, forming doctor of ministry candidates in certain kinds of practices that hopefully strengthen their ministries, then the process illustrates the faith the institutions that grant and cultivate doctor of ministry degrees still place in the medium we call dissertation. In a culture rapidly developing and proliferating media platforms, it is clear that a continued commitment to writing books, and reading books as preparation to write them, is an exercise in alternative reality. In an era "after the book," it is an exercise in keeping the trans- in trans-media, so that new media does not replace but rather layers older media. In this sense, the bookishness of the book-writing process is hospitable for the kind of contemplation necessary to raise awareness of media effects.

On the other hand, by studying media after the book, inclusive of the wide variety of media examined in this book, the very awareness raising that has happened redirects attention to the process of writing a book itself. It opens space to ask questions concerning the continuing validity and function of writing books in a trans-media era. It offers critical tools for doing so. However, having spent so many pages facilitating greater awareness of media effects for faith formation, perhaps the best conclusion is to invite readers, now having read the book, to ask to what degree and in what manner this book itself is subject to the kind of analysis exercised in the book. Like James Joyce's *Finnegan's Wake*, such an ending might send you back to the beginning to read it all over again, like a textual circle.

Bibliography

Adorno, Theodor. *Minima Moralia: Reflections from Damaged Life.* New York: Verso, 2005.

Augsburg Fortress Press. *Go Make Disciples: An Invitation to Baptismal Living: A Handbook to the Catechumenate.* Minneapolis: Augsburg Fortress, 2012.

———. *Welcome to Christ: A Lutheran Introduction to the Catechumenate.* Minneapolis: Augsburg Fortress, 1997.

Benjamin, Walter. *The Work of Art in the Age of Mechanical Reproducibility and OtherWritings on Media.* Cambridge, MA: Belknap Press, 2008.

Blascovich, Jim, and Jeremy Bailenson. *Infinite Reality: Avatars, Eternal Life, New Worlds, and the Dawn of the Virtual Revolution.* New York: HarperCollins, 2011.

Bogost, Ian. *Persuasive Games: The Expressive Power of Videogames.* Cambridge, MA: MIT Press, 2010.

Borgmann, Albert. *Power Failure: Christianity in the Culture of Technology.* Grand Rapids: Brazos, 2003.

boyd, danah. *Taken Out of Context.* PhD dissertation. University of California–Berkeley, 2008.

Brock, Brian. *Christian Ethics in a Technological Age.* Grand Rapids: Eerdmans, 2010.

Bruns, Axel. *Blogs, Wikipedia, Second Life and Beyond: From Production to Produsage.* New York: Peter Lang, 2008.

Carr, Nicholas. *The Shallows: What the Internet Is Doing to Our Brains.* New York: W. W. Norton, 2008.

Crouch, Andy. *Culture Making: Recovering Our Creative Calling.* Downers Grove, IL: InterVarsity, 2008.

Coupland, Douglas. *Marshall McLuhan: You Know Nothing of My Work!* New York: Atlas and Company, 2011.

De Certeau, Michel. *The Practice of Everyday Life.* Berkeley: University of California Press, 1984.

Dehaene, Stanislas. *Reading in the Brain: The New Science of How We Read.* New York: Penguin, 2009.

Detweiler, Craig. *Halos and Avatars: Playing Video Games with God.* Louisville: Westminster John Knox, 2010.

Dickerson, Matthew. *The Mind and the Machine: What It Means to Be Human and Why It Matters*. Grand Rapids: Brazos, 2011.

Doctorow, Cory. *Makers*. New York: Tor, 2010.

Edwards, Denis. *Breath of Life: A Theology of the Creator Spirit*. Maryknoll, NY: Orbis, 2004.

Estes, Douglas. *SimChurch: Being the Church in the Virtual World*. Grand Rapids: Zondervan, 2009.

Fowler, Robert M., Edith Blumhofer, and Fernando F. Segovia, eds. *New Paradigms for Bible Study: The Bible in the Third Millennium*. New York: T&T Clark, 2004.

Friesen, Dwight. *Thy Kingdom Connected: What the Church Can Learn from Facebook, the Internet, and Other Networks*. Grand Rapids: Baker, 2009.

Gee, James Paul. *What Video Games Have to Teach Us about Learning and Literacy*. 2nd ed. Hampshire, UK: Palgrave Macmillan, 2007.

Gibson, William. *Neuromancer*. New York: Ace, 2004.

Goody, Jack. *The Domestication of the Savage Mind*. Cambridge: Cambridge University Press, 1977.

Guder, Darrell. *Missional Church: A Vision for the Sending of the Church in North America*. Grand Rapids: Eerdmans, 1998.

Gorringe, T. J. *A Theology of the Built Environment: Justice, Empowerment, Redemption*. Cambridge: Cambridge University Press, 2002.

Halavais, Alexander. *Search Engine Society*. Cambridge, MA: Polity, 2009.

Harmless, William. *Augustine and the Catechumenate*. Collegeville, MN: Liturgical Press, 1995.

Hoffman, Paul. *Faith Forming Faith: Bringing New Christians to Baptism and Beyond*. Eugene, OR: Wipf and Stock, 2012.

Illich, Ivan. *In the Vineyard of the Text: A Commentary to Hugh's Didascalion*. Chicago: University of Chicago Press, 1993.

Innis, Harold A. *The Bias of Communication*. 2nd ed. Toronto: University of Toronto Press, 2008.

International Commission on English in the Liturgy. *The Rite of Christian Initiation of Adults*. Rev. ed. Collegeville, MN: Liturgical Press, 1988.

Jacobs, Alan. *The Pleasures of Reading in an Age of Distraction*. Oxford: Oxford University Press, 2011.

———. *Shaming the Devil: Essays in Truthtelling*. Grand Rapids: Eerdmans, 2005.

Jenkins, Henry. *Convergence Culture: Where Old and New Media Collide*. New York: New York University Press, 2006.

Jenson, Robert. *Essays in Theology of Culture*. Grand Rapids: Eerdmans, 1995.

———. *Systematic Theology, Volume One: The Triune God*. Oxford: Oxford University Press, 2001.

Johnson, Maxwell. *The Rites of Christian Initiation: Their Evolution and Interpretation*. Collegeville, MN: Liturgical Press, 1999.

Kärkkäinen, Veli-Matti. *Pneumatology: The Holy Spirit in Ecumenical, International, and Contextual Perspective*. Grand Rapids: Baker Academic, 2002.

MacIntyre, Alasdair. *After Virtue: A Study in Moral Theory*. Notre Dame, IN: University of Notre Dame Press, 2007.

McGonagal, Jane. *Reality Is Broken: Why Games Make Us Better and How They Can Change the World*. New York: Penguin, 2011.

McLuhan, Marshall. *The Medium Is the Massage*. Berkeley, CA: Gingko, 1967.

———. *Understanding Media: The Extensions of Man*. Corte Madera, CA: Gingko, 2003.

Moltmann, Jürgen. *The Spirit of Life*. Minneapolis: Fortress, 1992.

Murray, Iain H. *Jonathan Edwards: A New Biography*. Edinburgh: Banner of Truth Trust, 1987.

Pariser, Eli. *The Filter Bubble: What the Internet Is Hiding from You*. New York: Penguin, 2011.

Pettegree, Andrew. *The Book in the Renaissance*. New Haven, CT: Yale University Press, 2010.

Postman, Neil. *Amusing Ourselves to Death: Public Discourse in the Age of Show Business*. New York: Penguin, 2005.

Rushkoff, Douglas. *Program or Be Programmed: Ten Commands for a Digital Age*. Berkeley, CA: Soft Skull, 2010.

Satterlee, Craig. *Ambrose of Milan's Mystagogical Preaching*. Collegeville, MN: Liturgical Press, 2002.

Scharen, Christian, and Aana Marie Vigen. *Ethnography as Christian Theology and Ethics*. New York: Continuum, 2011.

Shirky, Clay. *Here Comes Everybody: The Power of Organizing without Organizations*. New York: Penguin, 2008.

Smith, James K. A. *Desiring the Kingdom: Worship, Worldview, and Cultural Formation*. Grand Rapids: Baker Academic, 2009.

Sontag, Susan. *On Photography*. New York: Picador, 1973.

Stephenson, Neal. *Anathem*. New York: Harper Perennial, 2010.

Sweet, Leonard. *Viral: How Social Networking Is Poised to Ignite Revival*. Colorado Springs: WaterBrook Press, 2012.

Thomas, Douglas, and John Seely Brown. *A New Culture of Learning: Cultivating the Imagination for a World of Constant Change.* New York: Create Space Independent Publishing Platform, 2011.

Turkle, Sherry. *Alone Together: Why We Expect More from Technology and Less from Each Other.* New York: Basic Books, 2011.

Ward, Pete. *Participation and Mediation: A Practical Theology for the Liquid Church.* London: SCM, 2008.

Weinberger, David. *Everything Is Miscellaneous: The Power of the New Digital Disorder.* New York: Holt Paperbacks, 2007.

Wolf, MaryAnne. *The Proust and the Squid: The Story and Science of the Reading Brain.* New York: HarperPerennial, 2007.

Websites

Adam, A. K. M. "Spirits in a Digital World." http://www.we-magazine.net/we-volume-02/spirits-in-a-digital-world/ (accessed January 20, 2012).

Forde, Gerhard O. "Radical Lutheranism." http://www.lutheranquarterly.com/Articles/ 2006/Special-Issue-20-Years/02-lq_forde.pdf (accessed January 16, 2012).

Lutheran Church of Honolulu. "Daily Prayer." http://www.lchwelcome.org/spirit/ office/office.php (accessed January 21, 2012).

Media Ecology Association."Media Ecology 101: An Introductory Reading List." http://www.media-ecology.org/media_ecology/readinglist.html (accessed January 16, 2012).

The New Atlantis, "Why Bother with Marshall McLuhan." http://www.thenewatlantis.com/publications/why-bother-with-marshall-mcluhan (accessed March 7, 2012).

St. Matthew's-by-the-Sea Chapel. "A Place for Peace for All in Second Life." http://stmattsinsl.wordpress.com (accessed January 16, 2012).

Index